ATLAS OF THE ARAB-ISRAELI CONFLICT

MARTIN GILBERT

Fellow of Merton College, Oxford

Macmillan Publishing Co., Inc.

NEW YORK

Macmillan Publishing Co., Inc.
866 Third Avenue, New York, N.Y. 10022
Collier-Macmillan Canada Ltd.

Library of Congress Cataloging in Publication Data

Gilbert, Martin, 1936-
Atlas of the Arab-Israeli conflict.

1. Near East—Historical geography—Maps. 2. Jews—Historical geography—Maps. 3. Arabs—Historical geography—Maps. 4. Jewish-Arab relations—History.
I. Title.

G2206.S1G5 911'.56 74-13917
ISBN 0-02-543370-9

Atlas of the Arab-Israeli Conflict was first published in 1974 in Great Britain as *The Arab-Israeli Conflict: Its History in Maps.*

First American Edition 1975

Printed in the United States of America

Preface

In this atlas I have traced the history of Arab-Jewish conflict from the turn of the century to the present day. I have tried to show something of the increasing intensity and bitterness of the conflict, of the types of incidents which it provoked, and of the views of those involved in it.

The majority of the maps in this atlas depict wars, conflict and violence, which have brought terrible suffering to all those caught up in them — Jew and Arab, soldier and civilian, adult and child. But there are also maps which show the various attempts to bring the conflict to an end, through proposals for agreed boundaries, through the signing of cease-fire agreements, and through negotiations. No map can show how peace will come, but they do show how much it is needed.

I am extremely grateful to Mr T.A. Bicknell, the cartographer, whose expertise has been invaluable, and who has dealt patiently with my many demands and amendments. I am also grateful to the many people who have provided me with factual material, who have scrutinized my drafts while they were being prepared, and who have given me the benefit of their professional knowledge and guidance. I should of course be grateful for readers' suggestions for further maps, for extra material, and for corrections.

Merton College   MARTIN GILBERT
Oxford
25 March 1974

Maps

ATLAS OF THE ARAB-ISRAELI CONFLICT

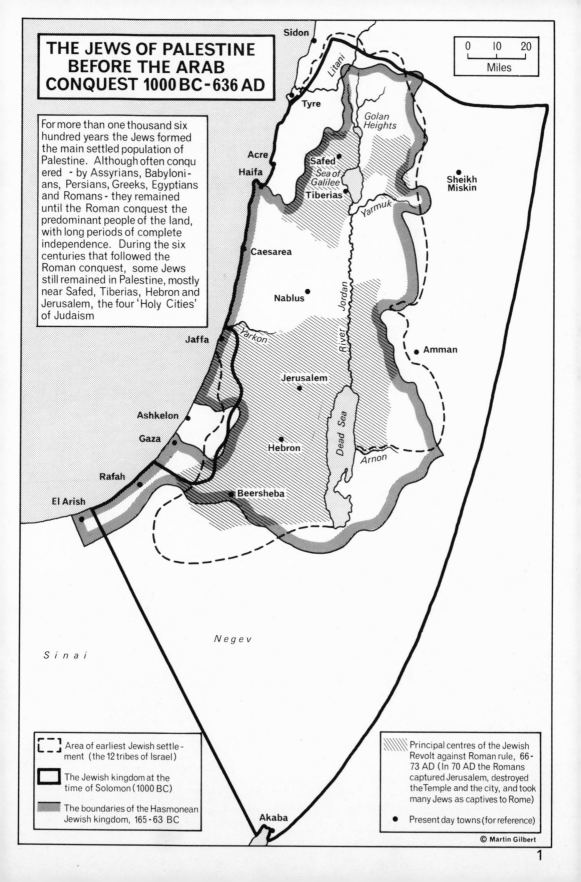

THE JEWS OF PALESTINE BEFORE THE ARAB CONQUEST 1000 BC - 636 AD

For more than one thousand six hundred years the Jews formed the main settled population of Palestine. Although often conquered - by Assyrians, Babylonians, Persians, Greeks, Egyptians and Romans - they remained until the Roman conquest the predominant people of the land, with long periods of complete independence. During the six centuries that followed the Roman conquest, some Jews still remained in Palestine, mostly near Safed, Tiberias, Hebron and Jerusalem, the four 'Holy Cities' of Judaism

0   10   20
Miles

Sidon

Litani

Tyre

Golan
Heights

Acre

Safed

Haifa

Sea of
Galilee

Sheikh
Miskin

Tiberias

Yarmuk

Caesarea

River Jordan

Nablus

Jaffa

Yarkon

Amman

Jerusalem

Ashkelon

Dead Sea

Gaza

Hebron

Arnon

Rafah

El Arish

Beersheba

Negev

Sinai

Akaba

```
┌ ─ ┐
└ ─ ┘  Area of earliest Jewish settle-
       ment (the 12 tribes of Israel)
```

The Jewish kingdom at the time of Solomon (1000 BC)

The boundaries of the Hasmonean Jewish kingdom, 165 - 63 BC

Principal centres of the Jewish Revolt against Roman rule, 66-73 AD (In 70 AD the Romans captured Jerusalem, destroyed the Temple and the city, and took many Jews as captives to Rome)

• Present day towns (for reference)

© Martin Gilbert

1

THE DISPERSAL OF THE JEWS,   100 – 300 AD

GERMANIA

Colonia

Rhine

Regina

Lutetia

Aquincu

PANNON

Genabum

G A L L I A

Alps

Vesontio

Tergeste

Burdigala

Genua

Ravenna

DALMATI

ITALIA

Tolosa

Pyrenees

Massilia

APULIA

CALAB

Roma

CAMPANIA

HISPANIA

SARDINIA

Corduba

Caralis

Gades

Panormus

SICILIA

Carthago

Volubilis

Melite

Atlas   Mountains

Sahara   Jews

Oea

S   A   H   A   R   A

Jews filled many occupations, being farmers and cattle raisers
(Mesopotamia), street traders (Egypt), slave-traders (Germany),
wine and olive-growers (Spain and North Africa), weavers,
garment-makers, actors, bakers and shipping-merchants
(Italy). They were equally active as agriculturalists and
town dwellers

By 300 A.D., the Jews had settled in every part of the Roman Empire except Britain. They were guaranteed freedom of religion and were allowed to practice Jewish law in disputes between Jews. They were exempt from military service.
There were probably at least three million Jews in 300 A.D., a million of whom lived west of Macedonia

0   200
Miles

Don

Tanais

Olbia

Mountain Jews

Phanagoria

Panticapaeum

Caucasus Mts.

rsa

Danube

Serdica   MOESIA

Trapezus

Amisus

Byzantium

Prusa   Ancyra

ASSYRIA

Tigris

MACEDONIA

Melitene   MESOPOTAMIA

PHRYGIA

Euphrates

Ephesus   Tarsus

CILICIA   Sura

Delos

Pumbedita

Babylon

ACHAIA   LYCIA   CYPRUS   SYRIA

Damascus

PALESTINA

Hierosolyma
(Jerusalem)

Cyrene

Alexandria

Berenice   Pelusium

Aelana

CYRENAICA   AEGYPTUS   *Sinai*

-dwelling
Jews

The 40,000 Jews of Cyprus were expelled after rebelling against Roman rule in 115 A.D.

■ Areas of widespread Jewish settlement by 300 A D

● Towns with large Jewish communities in 300 A D

◐ Isolated Jewish communities established after the Roman conquest of Palestine and preserving their Judaism for 16 centuries

© Martin Gilbert

JEWISH EXPULSIONS 1000 - 1500 AD

WALES

ENGLAND

1290

1290

Hamburg

Amsterdam

HOLLAND

Antwerp

FLANDERS

1290

Paris

1182

FRANCE

GERMANY

1306

1306

Udine

Venice

1420

1394

Turin

1394

PROVENCE

1394

Genoa

Livorno

ITALY

1490

Rome

1497

1492

NAVARRE

PORTUGAL

SPAIN

1492

1492

Naples

1497

1492

SARDINIA

1492

To
BRAZIL

1492

1492

Algiers

1492

SICIL

1492

Oran

Tunis

Fez

Tlemcen

Tripoli

M   A   G   H   R   E   B

■ Jewish communities with date of expulsion

→ Direction of the flight and dispersal of expelled Jews,
mostly to Poland, Italy and the Ottoman Empire

◉ Principal places of resettlement including Palestine

LITHUANIA

1445
1495
1495
1495

● Grodno
● Bialystok

RUSSIA

0   200
Miles

"O God, thou hast cast us off, thou hast scattered us, thou hast been displeased; O turn thyself to us again."
PSALM 60

192
● Posen
Kalisz ●
● Lodz
● Radom
Brest-Litovsk
● Pinsk
● Chernigov
● Kharkov

POLAND

SILESIA
1159
● Lublin
● Lutzk
● Kiev
Cracow
1494
● Lemberg
● Zhitomir
● Tarnopol

1350
1016
1016

...RIA
1421
● Kishinev

1016

HUNGARY
1349-1360

CRIMEA
Theodosia (Kaffa)

1016

1016
● Trebizond

● Nicopolis
Adrianople ●

● Spalato
● Cattaro

OTTOMAN

● Salonika

Constantinople

EMPIRE

CORFU ●

● Smyrna

● Aleppo

SYRIA

CRETE

● Damascus

● Safed
● Tiberias
● Jerusalem
PALESTINE
● Gaza

Alexandria

Cairo ●

OTTOMAN EMPIRE

© Martin Gilbert

THE JEWS OF PALESTINE
636 A.D. TO 1880

0 10 20 30
Miles

In 1500 there were an estimated 10,000 Jews living in the Safed region

1563 Establishment of a Hebrew printing press, the first printing press on the Asian Continent

1100 AD Jews take part in defence of Haifa against the Crusaders

Mediterranean Sea

1191 The Jews driven out by the Crusaders. Many move to Jerusalem

Jews sought a new homeland here after their expulsion from Spain (1492), Lithuania (1495), Portugal, Sicily and Sardinia (1497), Rhodes (1502) and Naples (1541)

1099 AD Jews take part in the defence of Jerusalem against the Crusaders, fighting alongside the Arabs
1211 Several rabbis from France and England settle here
1267 Ramban settles, and establishes a synagogue. During the next five centuries, Jerusalem is reinstated as a centre of Jewish learning. By 1880 the Jews formed the majority of the population of Jerusalem

24 Feb 1799 The Jewish community flees to Hebron on the eve of Napoleon's entry into the city

Tyre
Banias
Dan
Safed
Acre
Pekiin
Naveh
Haifa
Shefar Am
Sea of Galilee
Nazareth
Tiberias
Yarmuk River
Edrei
Caesarea
Beisan (Beit Shean)
Amatha
Nablus
Akraba
River Jordan
Jaffa
Ono
Bene Berak
Lod
Ramla
Yavne
Jerusalem
Ashkelon
Beit Guvrin
Hebron
Gaza
Yuttah
Dead Sea
Rafah
Beersheba
Zoar
Huseifa

The four 'Holy Cities' of Judaism, in which there was continuous Jewish settlement from biblical times

• Towns and settlements inhabited by Jews during the period of Arab rule from 637-1099

Area in which the Jews formed the main population from the thirteenth to the nineteenth century

◉ Towns and villages with continuous Jewish communities from the thirteenth to the nineteenth century

Jerusalem was conquered by Muslim Arabs in 637 AD. From 637 to 1099 the Arabs sometimes ill-treated and were sometimes tolerant towards their Jewish subjects. From 1099 to 1291 the Christian Crusaders mercilessly persecuted and slaughtered the Jews of Palestine. The Mameluks (Muslims) who ousted the Crusaders in 1291, and ruled until 1516, at times encouraged Jewish settlement, and many Jews came to Palestine to escape from Christian persecution in Europe. After 1517, under the Ottoman Turks the Jews of Europe continued to seek refuge in Palestine from Christian persecution and expulsion, despite spasmodic ill-treatment by their Muslim rulers

© Martin Gilbert

JEWISH SETTLEMENT IN PALESTINE 1880 – 1914

Between 1880 and 1914 over sixty thousand Jews entered Palestine, mostly from Russia, Galicia, Rumania and Poland. The victims of persecution and discrimination, they sought a new homeland and a new security under Turkish rule. Many settled on wasteland, sand-dunes and malarial marsh, which they then drained, irrigated and farmed. In 1909 a group of Jews founded the first entirely Jewish town, Tel Aviv, on the sandhills north of Jaffa. The Jews purchased their land piecemeal, from European, Turkish and (principally) Arab landlords, mostly at extremely high prices

Metulla

Yesod Hamaala

Ayelet Hashahar
Ein Zeitim
Mishmar Hayarden
Mahanayim
Safed
Rosh Pina

Acre

Haifa

Migdal
Kfar Hittim
Mizpa
Tiberias

Sea of Galilee

Bnei Yehuda

Sejera
Nazareth
Poriya
Kinneret
Sharona
Deganya
Kfar Tavor
Beitanya
Beit Gan
Menahemya
Yavneel

Atlit

Tantura

Shefeiya
Bat Shelomo
Zikhron Yaakov
Merhavya
Givat Ada
Beisan
Karkur
Heftzibah
Nahliel
Jenin
Gan Shmuel
Hadera

Tulkarm

Nablus

Kfar Mahal
Kfar Sava
Mikve Israel
Ein Hai
Petah Tikvah
Tel Aviv
Ein Ganim
Jaffa
Mahane Yehuda
Nahalat Yehuda
Ben Shemen
Ramallah
Rishon le Zion
Beer Yaakov
Ramla
Nes Ziona
Jericho
Rehovot
Ekron
Hulda
Motza
Gedera
Kfar Uriya
Jerusalem
Hartuv

Beer-Toviya (Kastinia)

Hebron

Gaza

Ruhama

Beersheba

APPROXIMATE POPULATIONS

1880:	470,000 Arabs
	24,000 Jews
1914:	500,000 Arabs
	90,000 Jews

Jordan

| 0 | 5 | 10 | 15 |

Miles

Between 1880 and 1903 over 25,000 Jews reached Palestine, mostly from Russia, and settled on the land. Between 1904 and 1914 a further 40,000 Jews arrived from eastern Europe, many of whom worked as hired labourers both on the land and in the towns. This 'second' Aliyah formed the first Jewish political parties in Palestine, and laid the foundations of a Hebrew press and modern Hebrew literature

Dead Sea

○ Arab towns with few, if any Jewish inhabitants by 1914

◉ Jewish settlements established between 1880 and 1914

● Towns with Jewish as well as Arab populations

© Martin Gilbert

5

ARAB-JEWISH CONFLICT UNDER TURKISH RULE 1882-1914

The reawakening of the Arab nation, and the growing Jewish efforts at rebuilding the ancient monarchy of Israel on a very large scale – these two movements are destined to fight each other continually, until one of them triumphs over the other.
NEGUIB AZOURY, LE REVEIL DE LA NATION ARABE PARIS 1905

In May and June 1914 anti-Zionist societies were established in Jerusalem, Jaffa, Haifa, Cairo, Beirut and Constantinople

```
0    10    20
Miles
```

Beirut

Damascus

BEIRUT

SANJAK OF DAMASCUS

Tyre

Huleh Swamp

Kuneitra

OF

Acre

Sea of Galilee

Haifa

SANJAK OF ACRE

Sejera

Kinneret

Nazareth

Yavniel

Degania

Mediterranean Sea

Merhaviya

Irbid

Hadera

Jenin

SANJAK OF AJLUN

Jordan River

VILAYET

SANJAK OF NABLUS

Salt

VILAYET OF DAMASCUS

Jaffa

Petah Tikva

Ness Ziona

Ben Shemen

Amman

Rehovot

Jerusalem

Gedera

MUTASARRIFLIK OF JERUSALEM

1891 Some Arab notables send a petition to Constantinople demanding the prohibition of Jewish immigration and Jewish land purchase

Hebron

Dead Sea

Gaza

Beersheba

Ports at which official measures were taken to prevent the entry of Jewish immigrants from Russia, Rumania and Bulgaria in 1882 (also Latakia)

Towns in which anti-Zionists newspapers were published by Arabs between 1908 and 1914, and which protested against Jewish land purchase

Jewish settlements attacked by Arab bands between 1886 and 1914

Principal administrative boundaries of the Turkish (Ottoman) Empire, as reorganised in 1888

Area in which Elias Sursuq of Beirut sold the Zionists 2,400 acres of potentially fine agricultural land, 1910-1911 despite protests in the Arab newspapers. The Jews paid high prices for all their land, although much of it was wasteland

·········· Administrative sub-divisions, 1888

© Martin Gilbert

6

BRITAIN'S PROMISE TO THE ARABS: 1915

0 — 5
Miles

Adana

Mersina

Alexandretta

Aleppo

VILAYET OF ALEPPO

Latakia

Hama

Homs

CYPRUS
British

Mediterranean Sea

Beirut

VILAYET OF BEIRUT

Sidon

Damascus

Acre

Safed

Haifa

VILAYET OF DAMASCUS

VILAYET

Hadera

Tel Aviv
Jaffa

Ramla

Amman

Jerusalem

Dead Sea

Gaza

Rafah

Beersheba

El Arish

MUTASARRIFLIK OF JERUSALEM

E G Y P T
British

Negev

Sinai

Taba — Akaba

▬ ▬ ▬ Line west of which Britain said 'should be excluded from the proposed limits and boundaries'of any future independent Arab State (McMahon's letter of 25 Oct 1915)

▨ Areas which the Sherif of Mecca declared to be 'purely Arab provinces', and wished to see as part of 'the pure Arab kingdom'. (Hussein's letter of 5 Nov 1915)

In 1915, in an attempt to win Arab support in the war against Turkey, Britain began negotiations with Hussein, Sherif of Mecca. On 25 Oct 1915 the British High Commissioner in Cairo, Sir H. McMahon, informed Hussein that Britain was 'prepared to recognize and support the independence of the Arabs....' But, he added, the Eastern Mediterranean littoral would have to be entirely excluded from any future Arab State. In his reply on 5 Nov 1915, Hussein insisted on the inclusion of the Vilayet of Beirut, but made no mention of the Mutasarriflik of Jerusalem. But on 14 Dec 1915 McMahon replied that any such inclusion 'will require careful consideration'. On 1 Jan 1916 Hussein warned McMahon: 'the people of Beirut will decidedly never accept such isolations'. At no point in the correspondence was any mention made of southern Palestine, Jerusalem or the Jews

© Martin Gilbert

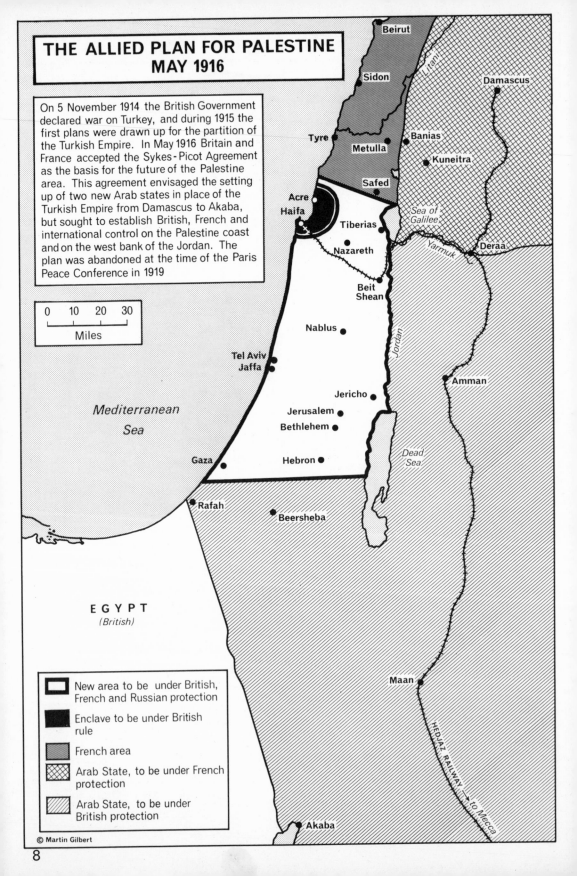

THE ALLIED PLAN FOR PALESTINE MAY 1916

On 5 November 1914 the British Government declared war on Turkey, and during 1915 the first plans were drawn up for the partition of the Turkish Empire. In May 1916 Britain and France accepted the Sykes-Picot Agreement as the basis for the future of the Palestine area. This agreement envisaged the setting up of two new Arab states in place of the Turkish Empire from Damascus to Akaba, but sought to establish British, French and international control on the Palestine coast and on the west bank of the Jordan. The plan was abandoned at the time of the Paris Peace Conference in 1919

```
0    10   20   30
|----|----|----|
      Miles
```

Beirut

Sidon

Damascus

Tyre

Litani

Banias

Metulla

Kuneitra

Safed

Acre

Haifa

Sea of Galilee

Tiberias

Deraa

Nazareth

Yarmuk

Beit Shean

Nablus

Jordan

Tel Aviv
Jaffa

Amman

Jericho

Mediterranean Sea

Jerusalem

Bethlehem

Gaza

Hebron

Dead Sea

Rafah

Beersheba

E G Y P T
(British)

Maan

HEDJAZ RAILWAY to Mecca

New area to be under British, French and Russian protection

Enclave to be under British rule

French area

Arab State, to be under French protection

Arab State, to be under British protection

Akaba

© Martin Gilbert

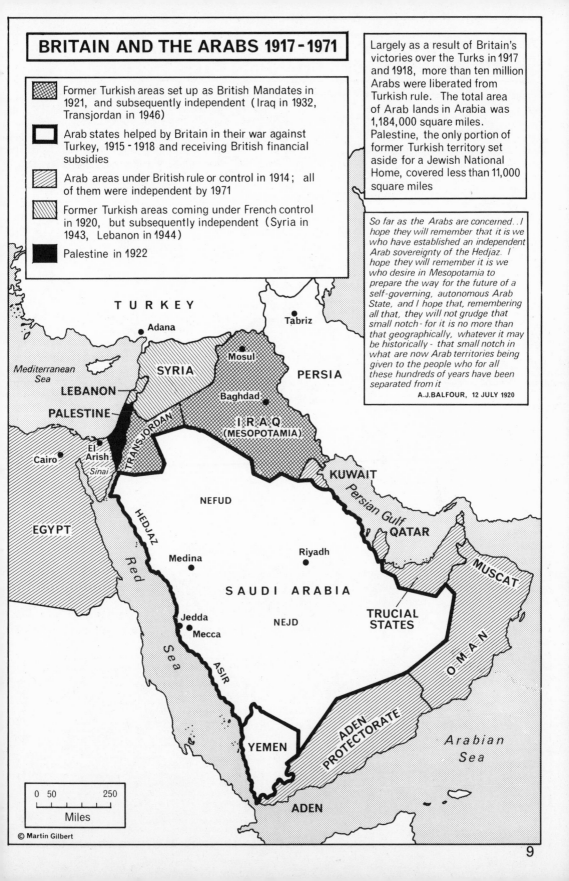

BRITAIN AND THE ARABS 1917-1971

Former Turkish areas set up as British Mandates in 1921, and subsequently independent (Iraq in 1932, Transjordan in 1946)

Arab states helped by Britain in their war against Turkey, 1915 - 1918 and receiving British financial subsidies

Arab areas under British rule or control in 1914; all of them were independent by 1971

Former Turkish areas coming under French control in 1920, but subsequently independent (Syria in 1943, Lebanon in 1944)

Palestine in 1922

Largely as a result of Britain's victories over the Turks in 1917 and 1918, more than ten million Arabs were liberated from Turkish rule. The total area of Arab lands in Arabia was 1,184,000 square miles. Palestine, the only portion of former Turkish territory set aside for a Jewish National Home, covered less than 11,000 square miles

So far as the Arabs are concerned..I hope they will remember that it is we who have established an independent Arab sovereignty of the Hedjaz. I hope they will remember it is we who desire in Mesopotamia to prepare the way for the future of a self-governing, autonomous Arab State, and I hope that, remembering all that, they will not grudge that small notch - for it is no more than that geographically, whatever it may be historically - that small notch in what are now Arab territories being given to the people who for all these hundreds of years have been separated from it

A.J.BALFOUR, 12 JULY 1920

TURKEY

Adana

Tabriz

Mediterranean Sea

SYRIA

Mosul

PERSIA

LEBANON

Baghdad

PALESTINE

TRANSJORDAN

IRAQ (MESOPOTAMIA)

Cairo

El Arish

Sinai

KUWAIT

Persian Gulf

NEFUD

QATAR

EGYPT

HEDJAZ

Red Sea

Medina

Riyadh

MUSCAT

SAUDI ARABIA

Jedda

Mecca

NEJD

TRUCIAL STATES

OMAN

ASIR

ADEN PROTECTORATE

Arabian Sea

YEMEN

0   50   250
Miles

ADEN

© Martin Gilbert

9

BRITAIN AND THE JEWISH NATIONAL HOME: PLEDGES AND BORDER CHANGES, 1917 – 1923

0   50
Miles

☐ The Palestine Mandate, granted to Britain at the San Remo Conference in 1920, as the region of a Jewish National Home

–·– Approximate boundary of the area in which the Jews hoped to set up their National Home

▨ Separated from Palestine by Britain in 1921, and given to the Emir Abdullah. Named Transjordan, this territory was at once closed to Jewish settlement

▨ Ceded by Britain to the French Mandate of Syria, 1923

His Majesty's Government view with favour the establishment in Palestine of a national home for the Jewish people, and will use their best endeavours to facilitate the achievement of this object, it being clearly understood that nothing shall be done which may prejudice the civil and religious rights of non-Jewish communities in Palestine or the rights and political status enjoyed by Jews in any other country THE BALFOUR DECLARATION 2 NOV 1917

The British conquered Palestine in 1917-1918, occupying Jerusalem in December 1917

Beirut

Sidon

Litani

Damascus

Tyre

Kuneitra   S Y R I A

Acre
Haifa   Safed   Sea of Galilee

Tiberias

Irbid

Mediterranean Sea

Nablus

River Jordan

Salt

Tel Aviv
Jaffa   Ramla

Ashkelon   Jerusalem   Amman

Bethlehem   Dead Sea

Gaza
Rafah

Kerak

Beersheba

El Arish

Negev

IRAQ

Suez Canal

E G Y P T

Petra

Maan

H E D J A Z
later SAUDI ARABIA

Eilat   Akaba

S i n a i

Gulf of Akaba

We Arabs, especially the educated among us, look with deepest sympathy on the Zionist movement.... We will wish the Jews a hearty welcome home.... We are working together for a reformed and revised Near East, and our two movements complement one another. The movement is national and not imperialistic. There is room in Syria for us both. Indeed, I think that neither can be successful without the other THE EMIR FEISAL TO FELIX FRANKFURTER 3 MARCH 1919

Makna

Strait of Tiran

If, as may well happen, there should be created in our own lifetime by the banks of the Jordan a Jewish State under the protection of the British Crown which might comprise three or four millions of Jews, an event will have occurred in the history of the world which would from every point of view be beneficial, and would be especially in harmony with the truest interests of the British Empire WINSTON CHURCHILL ILLUSTRATED SUNDAY HERALD 8 FEB 1920

Red Sea

© Martin Gilbert

10

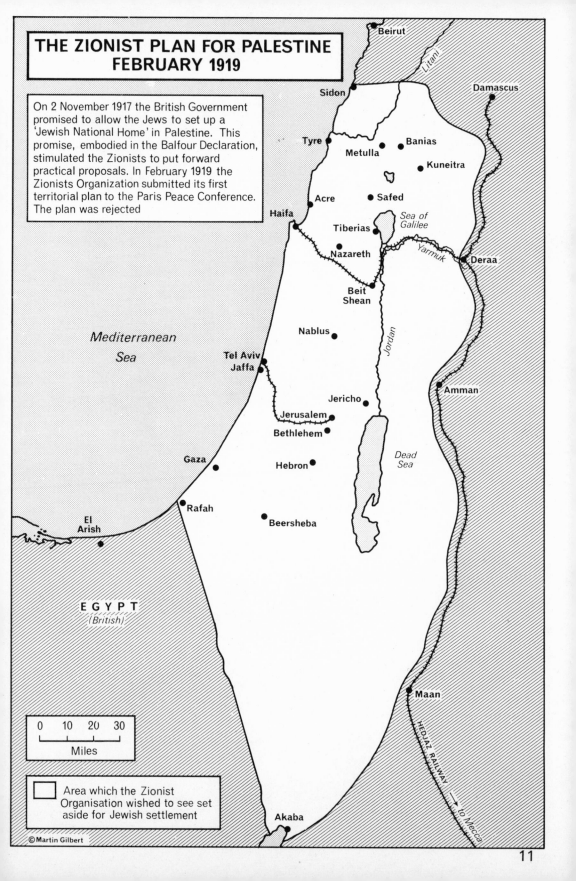

THE ZIONIST PLAN FOR PALESTINE FEBRUARY 1919

On 2 November 1917 the British Government promised to allow the Jews to set up a 'Jewish National Home' in Palestine. This promise, embodied in the Balfour Declaration, stimulated the Zionists to put forward practical proposals. In February 1919 the Zionists Organization submitted its first territorial plan to the Paris Peace Conference. The plan was rejected

Beirut

Litani

Sidon

Damascus

Tyre

Metulla
Banias

Kuneitra

Acre
Safed

Haifa
Sea of Galilee

Tiberias

Nazareth
Yarmuk
Deraa

Beit Shean

Mediterranean Sea

Nablus

Jordan

Tel Aviv
Jaffa

Amman

Jericho

Jerusalem

Bethlehem

Dead Sea

Gaza

Hebron

Rafah

El Arish

Beersheba

E G Y P T
(British)

Maan

| 0 | 10 | 20 | 30 |
Miles

HEDJAZ RAILWAY

to Mecca

Area which the Zionist Organisation wished to see set aside for Jewish settlement

Akaba

ARAB-JEWISH CONFLICT IN 1920

0 ____ 5
Miles

Mediterranean Sea

Metulla

Kfar Giladi   **Hamara**
Tel Hai
Halsa

Huleh Swamp

1 March 1920 In an attack by large numbers of Arabs from the village of Halsa, eight Jews were killed, among them Josef Trumpeldor, founder of the Russian Jewish pioneer movement (Hehalutz), which encouraged immigration to Palestine. Between 1919 and 1921 these four northernmost settlements were under French control

Ayelet Hashahar ⊙
Mishmar Hayarden ⊙
Mahanayim ⊙
Rosh Pina ⊙

Jordan

Acre

Haifa

June 1920 As a result of the Arab attacks in March and April, the Jews decided to set up their own defence force, the Haganah, to defend Jewish settlements from Arab attack

Sea of Galilee

Bnei Yehuda

Sharona ⊙
Kinneret
Kfar Tavor ⊙   Degania
Menahemya ⊙

Yarmuk

Dec 1920 The General Federation of Jewish Labour, the Histadrut, founded in order to encourage immigration, agricultural settlement, the growth of industry, and social welfare projects

25 April 1920 Following the murder by Arabs of a Jewish settler,   the whole settlement was abandoned. Unlike most of the other abandoned settlements, it was not resettled

Jordan

In 1919 and 1920 a total of over ten thousand Jewish immigrants entered Palestine, mostly from Russia. The Arabs feared that an eventual Jewish majority would destroy their chance of independent Arab statehood.
In September 1920, following the first Arab riots under British rule, the British authorities announced an upper limit to Jewish immigration of 16,500 a year

⊙   Jewish agricultural settlements attacked by armed Arab bands, March and April 1920

▬▬▬   Jewish settlements evacuated in 1920 as a result of repeated Arab attacks

© Martin Gilbert

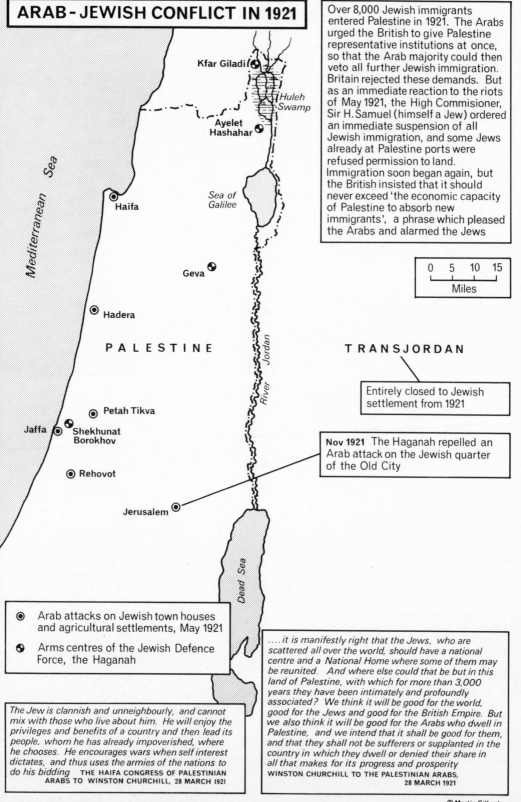

ARAB-JEWISH CONFLICT IN 1921

Over 8,000 Jewish immigrants entered Palestine in 1921. The Arabs urged the British to give Palestine representative institutions at once, so that the Arab majority could then veto all further Jewish immigration. Britain rejected these demands. But as an immediate reaction to the riots of May 1921, the High Commisioner, Sir H. Samuel (himself a Jew) ordered an immediate suspension of all Jewish immigration, and some Jews already at Palestine ports were refused permission to land. Immigration soon began again, but the British insisted that it should never exceed 'the economic capacity of Palestine to absorb new immigrants', a phrase which pleased the Arabs and alarmed the Jews

Kfar Giladi

Huleh Swamp

Ayelet Hashahar

Mediterranean Sea

Sea of Galilee

Haifa

Geva

Hadera

PALESTINE

River Jordan

TRANSJORDAN

Entirely closed to Jewish settlement from 1921

Petah Tikva

Jaffa
Shekhunat Borokhov

Nov 1921 The Haganah repelled an Arab attack on the Jewish quarter of the Old City

Rehovot

Jerusalem

Dead Sea

| 0 | 5 | 10 | 15 |

Miles

◉   Arab attacks on Jewish town houses and agricultural settlements, May 1921

✪   Arms centres of the Jewish Defence Force, the Haganah

....it is manifestly right that the Jews, who are scattered all over the world, should have a national centre and a National Home where some of them may be reunited. And where else could that be but in this land of Palestine, with which for more than 3,000 years they have been intimately and profoundly associated? We think it will be good for the world, good for the Jews and good for the British Empire. But we also think it will be good for the Arabs who dwell in Palestine, and we intend that it shall be good for them, and that they shall not be sufferers or supplanted in the country in which they dwell or denied their share in all that makes for its progress and prosperity
WINSTON CHURCHILL TO THE PALESTINIAN ARABS, 28 MARCH 1921

The Jew is clannish and unneighbourly, and cannot mix with those who live about him. He will enjoy the privileges and benefits of a country and then lead its people, whom he has already impoverished, where he chooses. He encourages wars when self interest dictates, and thus uses the armies of the nations to do his bidding THE HAIFA CONGRESS OF PALESTINIAN ARABS TO WINSTON CHURCHILL, 28 MARCH 1921

© Martin Gilbert

THE JEWISH SETTLEMENTS IN THE VALLEY OF JEZREEL 1921–1925

Principal Jewish settlements established in 1921 and 1922

ᔜᔛ Land over 500 feet

● Arab towns and villages

┼─┼─┼ The Haifa – Damacus railway

0 1 2 3 4
Miles

SYRIA

Sea of Galilee

Nazareth

Dabburiya

Nahalal

Mujeidil

Mt Tabor

to Haifa

Yarmuk

to Damacus

PALESTINE

Tel Adashim

Ginega

Tumrah

Balfouriya

Afula

Kfar Yehezkiel

Geva

Shatta

Ein Harod

Tel Yosef

Ezbuba

Salim

Sandala

El Mazur

Mukebila

Jalameh

Beit Alpha

Arana

Heftzibah

Beisan

Jenin

Mountains of Gilboa

Jezreel Valley

T R A N S J O R D A N

River Jordan

Between 1920 and 1925 the Jewish National Fund spent nearly a million Egyptian pounds buying land in the Valley of Jezreel. By 1925 over 2,600 Jews had settled in the valley, and 3,000 acres of barren hillside had been afforested. This previously uncultivated land, bought at highly inflated prices, became the pattern of all subsequent Jewish National Fund settlements in Palestine

When I first saw it in 1920 it was a desolation. Four or five small and squalid Arab villages, long distances apart from one another, could be seen on the summits of low hills here and there. For the rest, the country was unin-habited. There was not a house, not a tree…. about 51 square miles of the valley have now been purchased by the Jewish National Fund ….. Twenty schools have been opened. There is an Agricultural Training College for Women in one village and a hospital in another. All the swamps and marshes within the area that has been colonised have been drained …. The whole aspect of the valley has been changed…. in the spring the fields of vegetables or of cereals cover many miles of the land, and what five years ago was little better than a wilderness is being transformed before our eyes into smiling countryside. SIR H. SAMUEL'S REPORT ON THE ADMINISTRATION OF PALESTINE, 22 APRIL 1925

© Martin Gilbert

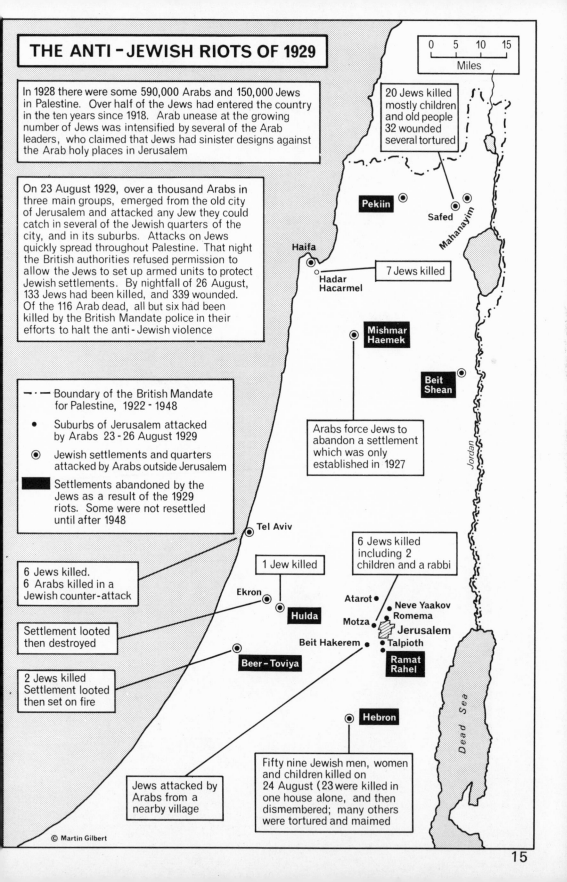

THE ANTI-JEWISH RIOTS OF 1929

In 1928 there were some 590,000 Arabs and 150,000 Jews in Palestine. Over half of the Jews had entered the country in the ten years since 1918. Arab unease at the growing number of Jews was intensified by several of the Arab leaders, who claimed that Jews had sinister designs against the Arab holy places in Jerusalem

On 23 August 1929, over a thousand Arabs in three main groups, emerged from the old city of Jerusalem and attacked any Jew they could catch in several of the Jewish quarters of the city, and in its suburbs. Attacks on Jews quickly spread throughout Palestine. That night the British authorities refused permission to allow the Jews to set up armed units to protect Jewish settlements. By nightfall of 26 August, 133 Jews had been killed, and 339 wounded. Of the 116 Arab dead, all but six had been killed by the British Mandate police in their efforts to halt the anti-Jewish violence

— · — Boundary of the British Mandate for Palestine, 1922 - 1948

● Suburbs of Jerusalem attacked by Arabs 23 - 26 August 1929

◉ Jewish settlements and quarters attacked by Arabs outside Jerusalem

▇ Settlements abandoned by the Jews as a result of the 1929 riots. Some were not resettled until after 1948

20 Jews killed mostly children and old people 32 wounded several tortured

Pekiin

Safed

Mahanayim

Haifa

Hadar Hacarmel

7 Jews killed

Mishmar Haemek

Beit Shean

Arabs force Jews to abandon a settlement which was only established in 1927

Jordan

Tel Aviv

6 Jews killed. 6 Arabs killed in a Jewish counter-attack

Settlement looted then destroyed

2 Jews killed Settlement looted then set on fire

1 Jew killed

Ekron

Hulda

Beer-Toviya

6 Jews killed including 2 children and a rabbi

Atarot
Neve Yaakov
Romema
Motza
Jerusalem
Beit Hakerem
Talpioth
Ramat Rahel

Hebron

Dead Sea

Jews attacked by Arabs from a nearby village

Fifty nine Jewish men, women and children killed on 24 August (23 were killed in one house alone, and then dismembered; many others were tortured and maimed

© Martin Gilbert

15

EUROPEAN ANTI-SEMITISM 1917–1933

© Martin Gilbert

300
0
Miles

PALESTINE
British Mandate

13,000 to Vladivostok and Harbin

1918. 900 Jews forced into the sea and drowned

1932. Ritual murder charge. Anti-Jewish riots

1917. Jewish schools and synagogues destroyed by fire

1918. Jewish elders massacred

WHITE RUSSIA

UKRAINE

Odessa

Yalta

Sebastopol

RUMANIA

BULGARIA

Kavalla

TURKEY

German Foreign Minister murdered: "Knock off Walter Rathenau the dirty god-damned Jewish sow."

POLAND

Auschwitz
Cracow
Lemberg

CZECHOSLOVAKIA

HUNGARY

YUGOSLAVIA

Salonika

GREECE

To U.S.A. and Latin America

Berlin 1922

1920–1933. Hitler preaches anti-semitism

Munich

AUSTRIA

GREAT BRITAIN

FRANCE

1933–1939. Small anti-semitic movements culminate in local anti-Jewish violence in imitation of Germany

SPAIN

Emancipation granted in 1930 but withdrawn by Franco in 1938

Area of anti-Jewish atrocities 1917–1921, mostly by anti-Bolshevik Russian armies. Over 100,000 Jews killed

The Flight of Jews 1917–1921

Towns in which specially organised Jewish Militias warded off anti-Jewish attacks 1918–1921

Countries in which Jewish rights were restricted, and anti-semitism flourished

THE JEWISH FLIGHT FROM PERSECUTION 1933–1941

SOVIET UNION

250,000

SWEDEN

BALTIC STATES

WHITE RUSSIA

DENMARK Hamburg 3,200

71,000

2,000

POLAND

GALICIA

UKRAINE

BESSARABIA

RUMANIA

SLOVAKIA

CZECHO

AUSTRIA

30,000
25,000
20,000
8,000
6,000
2,500

HUNGARY

YUGOSLAVIA 7,000

BULGARIA

GREECE 500,000

TURKEY

1941. 600 illegal immigrants

Beirut ● **LEBANON**

PALESTINE British Mandate

ISLE OF MAN Liverpool ●
GREAT BRITAIN
London ●

HOLLAND

BELGIUM

FRANCE

SWITZERLAND 25,000

12,000

3,000

15,000

Marseilles ●

Bilbao ●

Vigo ●

SPAIN

PORTUGAL

Lisbon ●

Oran ●

Casablanca ●

ITALY

- Ships with Jewish refugees whom the British Government refused to admit to Palestine. These ships were not allowed to land their human cargoes and sank. In all 600 Jews were drowned

- Ports through which 370,000 Jews fled to the Americas, 240,000 of them to the United States

- Rail and river routes by which 90,000 Jews reached Palestine, many entering illegally despite the British refusal to admit more than 75,000

1940 British Government interns 30,000 German and Austrian Jewish refugees as "enemy aliens"

1944. 8,000 Jewish children saved from death by being hidden in convents and private houses

Jews reaching Palestine 1939-44 from:-			
Poland	12,000	Yugoslavia	800
Rumania	8,000	Lithuania	600
Germany	8,000	USSR	600
Czechoslovakia	6,000	Italy	500
Hungary	3,000	France	300
Bulgaria	3,000	Holland	200
Greece	1,000	Latvia	100

	Greater Germany August 1939
	Refugees 1933–1941

To North and South America

0   200
Miles

©Martin Gilbert

17

ARAB FEARS OF A JEWISH MAJORITY IN PALESTINE
1920 - 1939

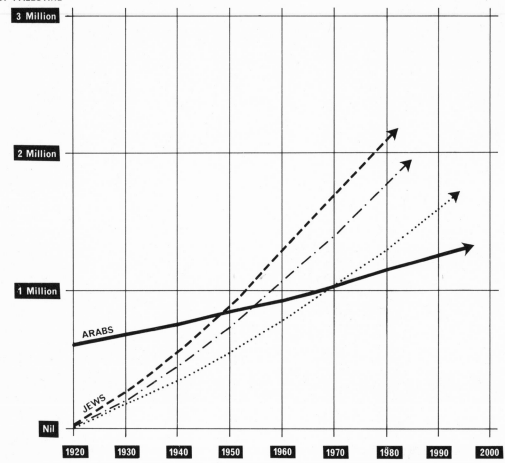

TOTAL POPULATION
OF PALESTINE

3 Million

2 Million

1 Million

ARABS

JEWS

Nil

1920　1930　1940　1950　1960　1970　1980　1990　2000

───── Estimated growth of the Arab population of Palestine, 1920-2000

– – – Estimated Jewish population, allowing for an annual immigration of 25,000 from 1930 (Jews would then equal Arabs by 1948)

–·–·– Estimated Jewish population, allowing for an annual immigration restricted to 15,000 (Jews would then equal Arabs by 1956)

··········· Estimated Jewish population, allowing for an annual immigration restricted to 10,000 (Jews would then equal Arabs by 1969)

These estimates were prepared by the British Government in 1929

As well as 360 000 Jewish immigrants between 1919 and 1939, over 50,000 Arabs also immigrated to Palestine (from nearby Arab States) attracted by the improving agricultural conditions and growing job opportunities, most of them created by the Jews

On the 17 May 1939, following a decade of Arab protest, the British Government issued a White Paper restricting Jewish immigration to 15,000 a year for five years, after which no immigration whatsoever would be allowed without Arab permission. The White Paper made it possible for the Arabs to prevent the Jews ever becoming a majority in Palestine

ROADS AND RIOTS IN PALESTINE 1921–1947

Because of the small number of paved roads in 1922, many Jewish settlements were remote, and thus vulnerable to Arab attack. As the road network spread between 1922 and 1947, these attacks concentrated on isolated settlements (many of them new ones) and on exposed sections of the roads. Most of the new roads built by the British after 1936 were planned in order to facilitate troop movements to outlying districts, the majority in areas of Arab rather than Jewish settlement, or to link Palestine with Egypt, Lebanon and Transjordan

━━━ Paved roads in 1922

─── New roads built by 1938

- - - New roads built by 1947

⊙ Jewish settlements attacked by Arabs in 1920, 1921, 1936-38 and 1947-48

Mediterranean Sea

LEBANON

to Beirut

Metulla

to Damascus

SYRIA

Acre

Haifa

Sea of Galilee

Jenin

TRANSJORDAN

Tubas

Nablus

River Jordan

Amman

Tel Aviv

Jaffa

Ramla

Ramallah

Jericho

Jerusalem

Dead Sea

Hebron

Gaza

Beersheba

Gevulot

EGYPT

to Kantara

Sinai

Negev

0 5 10 15

Miles

© Martin Gilbert

THE ARAB CAMPAIGN OF 1936: THE FIRST MONTH

0 5 10 15
Miles

—·—·— The British Palestine Mandate border, 1920-1948

▬▬▬ The Tel Aviv- Jerusalem road

1 May 1 Jew killed by Arabs, Arab killed by the police
2 May A second Jew dies as a result of the Arab attack of May 1
3 May An Arab mob burns down Jewish timber yard
13 May Jewish shops stoned by Arabs

11 May Arabs burn Jewish crops

4 May Jewish orchards burnt by Arabs
13 May More orchard fires

10 May Arabs uproot a newly planted olive grove
12 May Arabs burn out threshing floor

10 May Arabs burn crops & haystacks

19 April 7 Jews killed by Arabs. 2 Arabs killed by police
20 April 5 Jews killed by Arabs. 2 Arabs killed by police
21 April 2 Jews die from wounds received on 19 April
22 April 1 Jewish woman killed by Arabs

7 May Arabs fire on Jewish bus

4 May Arabs destroyed 200 acres of wheat

28 April 4 Jewish farmworkers injured by Arabs

26 April Jewish houses burnt by Arabs

29 April Arabs burn down a Jewish forest

15 April 2 Jews killed by Arabs

5 May Five hundred orange trees uprooted by Arabs

26 April An Arab mob beats up Jewish boy
29 April The police break up an Arab mob, wounding 9 Arabs
4 May 1 Arab killed by police
13 May 2 old Jews murdered by Arabs in the Old City

Haifa
Yagur
Ramat David
Migdal
Nazareth
Balfouriya
Zikhron Yaakov
Mishmar Ha-Emek
Beit Shean
Givat Ada
Tulkarm
Tel Mond
Jaffa
Beit Dagan
Jerusalem
Dead Sea

In the three years after Hitler came to power in 1933 the Jewish population of Palestine increased from 230,000 to 400,000 reaching one third of the Arab total. On 15 April 1936 the Arab began a General Strike followed by systematic attacks on Jewish lives, property and fields. On 7 May the Arab leaders met in Jerusalem, and demanded an end to all Jewish immigration, a halt to all Jewish land purchase, and an Arab majority Government. On 11 May, after three weeks of violence, the British authorities warned the Arabs that they intended to continue to 'suppress all outbreaks of lawlessness and punish the perpetrators'. On 13 May the Mufti of Jerusalem declared at Haifa: 'The Jews are trying to expel us from the country. They are murdering our sons and burning our houses'. Within a month of the first Jewish death, 21 Jews had been killed, and many farms and orchards burned by Arab action. 6 Arabs had been killed by the police, none by the Jews

© Martin Gilbert

THE ARAB CAMPAIGN 1936: THE SECOND MONTH

As the Arab riots continued for a second month, the British authorities began to take more active measures, in the course of which 10 Arabs were killed. The Arabs killed a further 7 Jews, destroyed over 15,000 Jewish trees, and burnt many crops and barns. It has not been possible to show every incident on this map

- – - – The British Palestine Mandate border, 1920-1948

━━━━ The Tel Aviv - Jerusalem road

24 May Arabs severely wound a Jewish watchman

13 June Arabs destroy Jewish crops

24 May Arabs uproot 1,200 Jewish citrus trees

30 May Jewish wheatfields burnt

28 May 3 Arab 'brigands' killed by British troops

23 May Arab mob stones the police
30 May 1 Arab killed by British during arms raid

5 June 5 Jewish passengers injured when Arabs threw bomb at bus
6 June 1 Arab killed by police during an anti-Jewish demonstration

30 May Arabs uproot 2,000 Jewish trees

30 May Arabs burn several hundred Jewish fruit trees

28 May 3,000 Jewish trees uprooted by Arabs
30 May A further 2,000 trees uprooted

6 June 650 Jewish trees uprooted by Arabs

6 June Arabs uproot 1,700 Jewish trees

20 May Jewish crops burnt by Arabs

16 May Police kill 1 Arab after an anti-Jewish demonstration
28 May 1 Arab rioter killed by a British policeman
30 May 2 Arabs killed by British

16 May 3 Jews shot dead by Arabs while coming out of a cinema
18 May Arabs kill an Austrian Christian (by mistake)
19 May Arabs kill a Jew in the Old City
25 May Arabs kill a Jew at the Hebrew University
28 May Arabs kill a British policeman in the Old City
31 May 1 Jew killed by Arabs at Givat Shaul

8 June Arabs attack Jews on their way to the Dead Sea Potash works

Majd el Krum

Haifa

Sejera

Yokneam

Yavniel

Balfouriya

Mishmar Ha-Emek

Karkur

Jenin

Hadera

Tel Mond

Nablus

Petah Tikva

Tel Aviv
Jaffa

Bab el-Wad

Givat Shaul

Mount Scopus

Motza

Jerusalem

Gaza

Dead Sea

25 May Arabs destroy Jewish vegetable crop 1 Arab killed by police
6 June Arabs uproot 2,400 Jewish trees

1 June A Jewish passenger killed by Arab rifle fire in a bus on its way from Jerusalem to Tel Aviv

20 May 2 Jews wounded during an Arab attack on the Jerusalem-Tel Aviv bus

6 June 1 Jewish girl severely injured by Arab fire while travelling by bus

© Martin Gilbert

21

THE ARAB CAMPAIGN OF 1936: THE THIRD MONTH

During the third month of the Arab campaign, the British took even firmer action, killing 22 Arab rioters. During the same period the Arabs destroyed over 75,000 Jewish trees, and extended their attacks to Jewish vineyards. Nine Jews were killed, mostly in Arab ambushes on buses. On 9 July the Arab Supreme Council again demanded a total halt to Jewish immigration

--·-- The British Palestine Mandate border, 1920-1948

▬▬ The Tel Aviv - Jerusalem road

16 June Arabs desecrate the tomb of the prophet Hosea
14 July British troops killed 2 Arabs rioters

23 June 1 Jew killed by 2 Arab rioters

Rosh Pina

Safed

29 June A Jewish watchman killed by Arabs

27 June Arabs destroy 3,500 Jewish grape vines
1 July 1 Jewish guard killed by Arabs
17 July 1 Jew killed by Arabs

Zikhron Yaakov

Jenin

13 July British troops kill 7 Arab 'gunmen'

Hadera

10 July 1 Jew killed on the Jenin-Nablus road when Arabs ambush bus

Anabta

16 June 2,000 Jewish orange trees and grape vines destroyed

Kfar Yona

17 July British troops kill 6 Arabs

Nablus

7 July 1 Jew killed in an Arab attack

25 June 1 British soldier and 6 Arabs killed when the British Army tried to halt an Arab riot
5 July British troops kill 1 Arab rioter

Tel Aviv

16 June Arabs uproot 1,000 fruit trees

Ramla
Ness Ziona

Ataroth

25 June 1 Jew killed by Arabs

Jerusalem

Motza

5 July 1 Jew killed by an Arab bomb

28 June 1 Jew seriously wounded by Arabs

9 July A 16 year old Jewish boy killed in an Arab ambush

Following a strong debate among the Jews, the Jewish Defence Force, the Haganah, declared a policy of restraint and non-retaliation. This policy was strictly imposed by the Haganah, who brought to trial anyone who sought to break it

It is true of course that in times of disturbance the Jews, as compared with the Arabs, are the law-abiding section of the population, and indeed, throughout the whole series of outbreaks, and under very great provocation, they have shown a notable capacity for discipline and self-restraint
PALESTINE ROYAL COMMISSION REPORT, JULY 1937, p. 121

0   10   20
Miles

© Martin Gilbert

THE ARAB CAMPAIGN OF 1936: THE CLIMAX

0 5 10 15 20
Miles

–·– The British Palestine Mandate border 1920-1948

—— The Tel Aviv - Jerusalem road

28 July Arab sniper kills a Jew
15 Aug 4 Jews killed by Arabs using dum-dum bullets
13 Sept 2 British soldiers killed by Arab tanks

2 Aug 2 Jewish guards shot dead by Arabs using dum-dum bullets

18 Aug Arabs kill 50 Jewish cattle

6 Aug Jewish settler murdered

1 Sept Jewish truck driver killed in ambush

20 July Arabs kill Jewish watchman

25 Aug Jewish bus driver killed by Arabs

7 Aug Arab sniper kills Jew
16 Aug Jewish boy killed by Arab bomb
17 Aug 2 Jewish nurses and one young Jewish girl killed by Arabs
22 Aug Two Jews killed
27 Aug An Arab wounded as reprisal

12 Oct Jewish policeman killed

15 Aug Arab ambush kills Jew on bus

13 Aug A Jewish father and his 3 children killed by an Arab bomb thrown through the window of their home

19 Sept Arab bomb kills 7 year old Jewish child
22 Sept Jewish watchman killed

11 Aug Arabs kill Jewish watchman

12 Aug Arabs kill a British soldier while he is bathing

26 Aug 2 Jewish watchman killed in Arab-British crossfire

22 July 1 British soldier killed in Arab ambush

29 July 5 Arabs killed by British soldiers

28 July 1 British constable, 10 Arabs killed in British-Arab battle

29 July Arabs kill a Jewish watchman
13 Aug Arabs kill another watchman
22 Aug 4 Jews killed by Arabs while driving from Tel Aviv

23 July 9 Jewish children injured in Arab bomb attack on religious school

22 Aug Lewis Billig, a Jewish Professor of Arabic Literature, murdered by Arabs. One obituary pointed out: 'He was working on the very culture the Arabs have lost'.

26 July British troops kill 12 Arab snipers

20 Aug Jewish taxi driver murdered by Arabs

3 Aug 1 Jew killed in Arab ambush

Map locations: Safed, Haifa, Tiberias, Mitzpa, Yokneam, Beit Alpha, Beit Shean, Hadera, Hogla, Netanya, Kafr el Labad, Tulkarm, Even Yehuda, Nablus, Kfar Saba, Sarona, Tel Aviv, Jaffa, Ramla, Bab el-Wad, Jerusalem, North Talpioth, Kfar Etzion

From mid-July, Arab attacks on Jews increased. Many Jews were ambushed and killed while driving, unarmed, on the main roads. Between 20 July and 22 September, 33 Jews were killed, and several hundred injured. At the same time, the British army was engaged in continuous battles with bands of armed Arabs, killing over 100 Arabs between 15 July and 3 October. During the same period, the Arabs killed 33 British soldiers. The Arab aim according to an Arab spokesman on 22 September was to 'extend the guerilla warfare against British troops', in order to bring 'an end to Zionist influence in London'. The Arabs called off their strike on October 12. In all 80 Jews had been killed

© Martin Gilbert

23

THE PEEL COMMISSION PARTITION PLAN, JULY 1937

In April 1936, following repeated Arab attacks against Jewish life and property, the British Government appointed a Royal Commission to enquire into the working of the Mandate. In July 1937 the Commission issued its Report, recommending the Partition of Palestine into two separate states, one Jewish and one Arab, with a British controlled corridor from Jaffa to Jerusalem. The Jews, reluctantly accepted this plan. The Arabs rejected it.

LEBANON

SYRIA

Damascus

Metulla

Sea of
Galilee

Acre
Haifa

Tiberias

Deraa

Afula

Beit
Shean

*Mediterranean
Sea*

Nablus

Jerash

Tel Aviv
Jaffa

Petah
Tikva

Ramallah

Amman

Rehovot

Lod
Ramla

Jericho

Jerusalem

Bethlehem

*Dead
Sea*

Gaza

Hebron

T R A N S -
J O R D A N

El Arish

N e g e v

```
0   10   20   30
Miles
```

Petra

Maan

- ⋅ — The frontier of the Palestine Mandate

▮ The proposed Jewish State, 1937

▨ The proposed Arab State, 1937.
Transjordan was already barred to
Jewish settlement

▭ The proposed area to remain
under British control

Akaba

© Martin Gilbert

24

THE PROPOSED JEWISH STATE: A TERRITORIAL COMPARISON

■ The size of the Jewish State proposed by the Peel Commision, 1937

□ Great Britain on the same scale

'It is our belief that a great Jewish community, a free Jewish nation, in Palestine, with a large scope for its activities, will be of great benefit to our Arab neighbours... We need each other, We can benefit each other'

DAVID BEN GURION TO THE PEEL COMMISSION, 7 JANUARY 1937

'Every Arab in Palestine will do everything in his power to crush down Zionism, because Zionism and Arabism can never be united together'

AWNI BEY ABDULHADI TO THE PEEL COMMISSION 13 JANUARY 1937

This map is based upon a map specially prepared for the Peel Commissioners before they left London for Palestine

WALES

Birmingham

Cambridge

Haifa

Oxford

London

Reading

Tel Aviv

Jerusalem

Southampton

Eastbourne

0   25   50
Miles

© Martin Gilbert

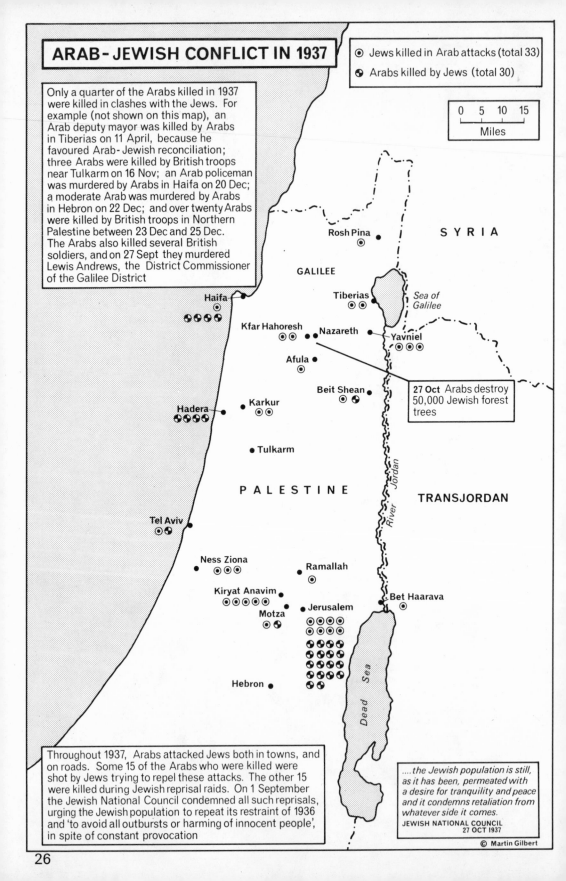

ARAB - JEWISH CONFLICT IN 1937

⊙ Jews killed in Arab attacks (total 33)
✪ Arabs killed by Jews (total 30)

0 5 10 15
Miles

Only a quarter of the Arabs killed in 1937 were killed in clashes with the Jews. For example (not shown on this map), an Arab deputy mayor was killed by Arabs in Tiberias on 11 April, because he favoured Arab-Jewish reconciliation; three Arabs were killed by British troops near Tulkarm on 16 Nov; an Arab policeman was murdered by Arabs in Haifa on 20 Dec; a moderate Arab was murdered by Arabs in Hebron on 22 Dec; and over twenty Arabs were killed by British troops in Northern Palestine between 23 Dec and 25 Dec. The Arabs also killed several British soldiers, and on 27 Sept they murdered Lewis Andrews, the District Commissioner of the Galilee District

SYRIA

Rosh Pina ⊙

GALILEE

Tiberias ⊙⊙   *Sea of Galilee*

Haifa ⊙
✪✪✪✪

Kfar Hahoresh ⊙⊙   Nazareth   Yavniel ⊙⊙⊙

Afula ⊙

Beit Shean ⊙✪

27 Oct Arabs destroy 50,000 Jewish forest trees

Hadera
✪✪✪✪

Karkur ⊙⊙

Tulkarm

PALESTINE

TRANSJORDAN

River Jordan

Tel Aviv ⊙✪

Ness Ziona ⊙⊙⊙

Ramallah ⊙

Kiryat Anavim ⊙⊙⊙⊙⊙

Bet Haarava

Motza ⊙✪   Jerusalem ⊙⊙⊙
⊙⊙⊙⊙
✪✪✪✪
✪✪✪✪
✪✪✪✪
✪✪

Hebron

Dead Sea

Throughout 1937, Arabs attacked Jews both in towns, and on roads. Some 15 of the Arabs who were killed were shot by Jews trying to repel these attacks. The other 15 were killed during Jewish reprisal raids. On 1 September the Jewish National Council condemned all such reprisals, urging the Jewish population to repeat its restraint of 1936 and 'to avoid all outbursts or harming of innocent people', in spite of constant provocation

....the Jewish population is still, as it has been, permeated with a desire for tranquility and peace and it condemns retaliation from whatever side it comes.
JEWISH NATIONAL COUNCIL
27 OCT 1937

© Martin Gilbert

ARAB - JEWISH CONFLICT MAY - JULY 1938

25 May 1 Arab killed
6 July Jewish terrorists kill 25 Arabs. Arabs kill 5 Jews
10 July 2 Jews killed
11 July 2 Jews killed
12 July An old Jew stoned to death
25 July Jewish terrorists kill 39 Arabs in the Melon market. 2 Jews killed later in the day

13 July 1 Jew killed

5 June 1 Jewish watchman killed

21 July Large Arab band kills five Jews, including 2 children
25 July 1 Jew killed

21 July An Arab band attacks Jewish vineyards. 1 Jew and 8 Arabs killed

4 May 1 Jew badly wounded

18 May Three thousand citrus trees destroyed by a band of 50 Arabs (600 trees had been destroyed in 1934)
18 June 5 Arabs killed while attacking the Jewish settlement
17 July 1 Jew killed

23 June 2 Jews and 2 Arabs killed
25 June 1 Jew killed
17 July 1 Jew killed

10 May Settlers repel attack by more than 20 Arabs
22 May 1 Jew killed in Arab attack
8 June 2 Jews killed
1 July 1 Jewish watchman killed

2 July 1 Jewish watchman killed
26 July 2 Jews killed (a father and his son). Two Arab attackers killed

5 July Five Jews killed

8 June 1 Jew killed

14 May Arabs destroy 25 dunams of orange groves

14 May Arab attack repulsed

25 July One Jew killed

11 June Arabs kill a Jewish watchman

13 June Jews repulse an Arab attack. 1 Arab killed

20 June 1 Jewish watchman killed

14 May Arab attack repulsed

14 May Arab attack repulsed
10 July Arabs kill 2 Jews

18 June 1 Jewish railway foreman killed

6 June Arabs burn 25 dunams of Jewish crops
17 July 1 Jew killed
19 July 1 Jew killed

21 July A band of 20 Arabs kill 4 Jewish labourers

22 May 1 Jew killed
24 May 1 Jew, 1 Christian and 1 Arab killed. The Jews Community Council urges restraint
12 June A Jewish carpenter murdered: the murderer flees to Arab village of Deir Yassin
4 July Four Arabs killed
5 July One Jew killed
7 July Two Arabs killed
15 July Jewish terrorists kill ten Arabs
26 July One Jew killed

4 July 1 Arab killed
17 July 3 Arabs and 1 Jew killed

21 July 1 Jew killed

Mishmar Hayarden
Hanita
Rosh Pina
Safed
Migdal
Kfar Hittim
Haifa
Ramat Yohannan
Mitzpa
Nahalal
Tiberias
Kiryat Haroshet
Gvat
Zikhron Yaakov
Geva
Givat Ada
Nir David
Karkur
Hadera
Tulkarm
Kfar Saba
Tel Aviv
Jaffa
Motza
Jerusalem
Ein Fashkha

The Arab campaign continued throughout 1938 and 1939. Partly intended as a protest against Britain for allowing Jewish immigration, its main efforts were aimed against Jewish settlements, and Jewish road traffic. At this time a small group of Jewish extremists began to commit regular terrorist acts. This map shows the principal Arab-Jewish incidents in the three months between May and July 1938, when 59 Jews were killed by Arabs, and 102 Arabs by Jews. Most of the Arabs were killed in three bomb attacks by Jewish terrorists. Most of the Jews were killed singly, during Arab attacks on scattered and isolated settlements. The frequent clashes between Arab bands and British troops are not shown; nor are the many occasions on which Arabs were killed by Arabs

© Martin Gilbert

A JEWISH PROPOSAL FOR PARTITION, 1938

0 5 10 15
Miles

Following the Peel Commission's Report, the Jewish Agency put forward its own partition plan. The Agency was prepared to see an Arab State on the West Bank of the Jordan, and in the Gaza-Beersheba area. It also contemplated the division of Jerusalem between the Jewish State and a Mandated territory

We are of the opinion that Galilee should not be included in the Jewish State.... the population is almost entirely Arab and the land is almost entirely owned by Arabs.... the Arabs in Galilee are vehemently opposed to the inclusion of that area in a Jewish State; they will certainly resist such inclusion by force
WOODHEAD COMMISSION REPORT 19 OCT 1938 COMMENT ON JEWISH PLAN

Metulla

☐ Proposed Jewish State (in two sections)

▨ Proposed Arab State (in three sections, including Jaffa)

▨ To remain under British Mandate

Safed

Acre

GALILEE

Sea of Galilee

Haifa

Mediterranean Sea

Nazareth

Afula

Beit Shean (Beisan)

Jenin

Natanya

Tulkarm

Nablus

PART OF THE PROPOSED **ARAB STATE**

Tel Aviv

Jaffa

Bayit Vegan

Rishon le Zion

Ramla

Rehovot

Ramallah

Jericho

Kallia

Jerusalem

Bethlehem

Faluja

Hebron

Gaza

Khan Yunis

Rafah

Beersheba

Jordan

The population consists of about 7,000 Arabs and about 200 Jews. It is an area capable of development. It contains a large number of springs, and water which at present is not being used economically.... it is undesirable that the town of Beisan, which is an entirely Arab town with over 3,000 inhabitants and a centre of Arab nationalism, should be included in the Jewish State
WOODHEAD COMMISSION REPORT COMMENT ON JEWISH PLAN

Dead Sea

....no impartial person would think the Arabs justified in claiming sovereign rights over persons and property of Jews who have settled in other parts of Palestine on the faith of the Balfour Declaration and the Mandate
WOODHEAD COMMISSION REPORT

© Martin Gilbert

28

A BRITISH PLAN FOR PARTITION, 1938

0 5 10 15
Miles

The Peel Commission of 1937 had recommended the partition of Palestine into separate Jewish and Arab States. The Woodhead Commission of 1938 examined in detail several partition proposals. This map shows their Plan B, under which the Jewish State would contain 300,400 Jews and 188,400 Arabs (of whom 50,000 lived in the Haifa region). In the Jerusalem-Bethlehem-Ramallah area 90,000 Arabs and 76,000 Jews would remain under British rule

- Proposed Jewish State (in two sections)
- Proposed Arab State (plus Jaffa)
- To remain under British Mandate
- Jewish owned land which would be inside the Arab State under this plan

It has been alleged that the Jews have acquired the best land in Palestine. It does not appear to me a fair statement. That much of the land now in possession of Jews has become the best land is a truer statement... It was impossible not to be impressed when inspecting some of the bare rocky places where Jewish settlements have been or are in the course of being made. Such remarkable efforts may well disturb statistics.
MINORITY REPORT, WOODHEAD COMMISSION REPORT, 19 OCT 1938

PART OF THE PROPOSED **ARAB STATE**

Metulla

Hanita
Nahariya
Safed
Acre
GALILEE
Sea of Galilee
Haifa
Tiberias
Nazareth
Afula
Jenin
Beit Shean (Beisan)
Tulkarm
Netanya
Nablus
River Jordan
Tel Aviv
Jaffa
Bayit Vegan
Rishon le Zion
Ramla
Rehovot
Ramallah
Jericho
Kallia
Jerusalem
Bethlehem
Mediterranean Sea
Faluja
Hebron
Dead Sea
Gaza
Khan Yunis
Rafah
Beersheba

© Martin Gilbert

THE JEWS OF EUROPE 1937-1941

Germany in 1937: less than 5% of European Jewry

Countries from which Jews were sent to concentration camps. All these countries were independent in 1937 and fell under German control or influence 1938-1941. Figures show Jewish populations in 1937 and percentage of total population (Germany 0.8%)

Countries neutral or unconquered 1939-1945 from which no Jews were sent to their death

PALESTINE
JEWISH IMMIGRATION VIRTUALLY PROHIBITED BY BRITAIN AFTER MAY 1939

© Martin Gilbert

CENTRAL RUSSIA
900,000

TURKEY
75,000
4%

UKRAINE
1,700,000
2.8%

WHITE RUSSIA
400,000

ESTONIA
5,000
0.4%

LATVIA
94,000
5.4%

LITHUANIA
160,000
7.6%

FINLAND
2,000
0.04%

SWEDEN
10,000
0.16%

MEMEL
3,000

DANZIG
7,000

POLAND
3,275,000
10.5%

CZECHOSLOVAKIA
360,000 2.5%

HUNGARY
440,000
5.6%

AUSTRIA
180,000
2.5%

RUMANIA
800,000
4.8%

BULGARIA
50,000
0.8%

YUGOSLAVIA
75,000
0.6%

ALBANIA

GREECE
75,000
1.2%

NORWAY
2,000
0.05%

DENMARK
7,000
0.17%

GERMANY
365,000

HOLLAND
115,000
2.2%

BELGIUM
44,000
0.8%

LUXEMBOURG
3,000
0.6%

FRANCE
270,000
0.4%

SWITZERLAND
20,000
1.6%

ITALY
50,000
0.12%

BRITAIN
340,000
0.7%

EIRE
5,000

PORTUGAL
3,000
0.02%

SPAIN
5,000
0.02%

GIBRALTAR
1,000
8.1%

0   200
Miles

30

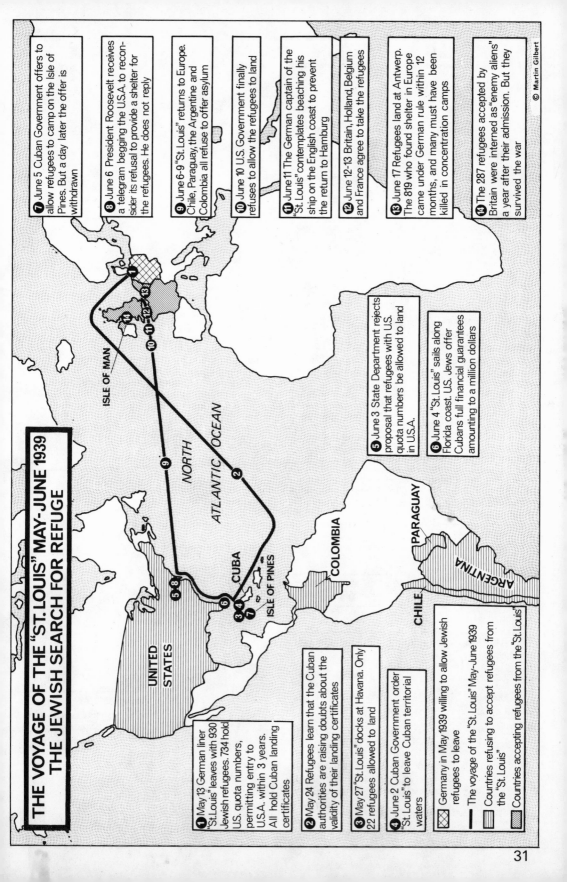

THE VOYAGE OF THE "ST. LOUIS" MAY-JUNE 1939 THE JEWISH SEARCH FOR REFUGE

1 May 13 German liner "St.Louis" leaves with 930 Jewish refugees. 734 hold U.S. quota numbers, permitting entry to U.S.A. within 3 years. All hold Cuban landing certificates

2 May 24 Refugees learn that the Cuban authorities are raising doubts about the validity of their landing certificates

3 May 27 "St.Louis" docks at Havana. Only 22 refugees allowed to land

4 June 2 Cuban Government order "St. Louis" to leave Cuban territorial waters

5 June 3 State Department rejects proposal that refugees with U.S. quota numbers be allowed to land in U.S.A.

6 June 4 "St. Louis" sails along Florida coast. U.S. Jews offer Cubans full financial guarantees amounting to a million dollars

7 June 5 Cuban Government offers to allow refugees to camp on the Isle of Pines. But a day later the offer is withdrawn

8 June 6 President Roosevelt receives a telegram begging the U.S.A. to reconsider its refusal to provide a shelter for the refugees. He does not reply

9 June 6-9 "St. Louis" returns to Europe. Chile, Paraguay, the Argentine and Colombia all refuse to offer asylum

10 June 10 U.S. Government finally refuses to allow the refugees to land

11 June 11 The German captain of the "St. Louis" contemplates beaching his ship on the English coast to prevent the return to Hamburg

12 June 12-13 Britain, Holland, Belgium and France agree to take the refugees

13 June 17 Refugees land at Antwerp. The 819 who found shelter in Europe came under German rule within 12 months, and many must have been killed in concentration camps

14 The 287 refugees accepted by Britain were interned as "enemy aliens" a year after their admission. But they survived the war

ISLE OF MAN

NORTH ATLANTIC OCEAN

UNITED STATES

CUBA

ISLE OF PINES

COLOMBIA

PARAGUAY

CHILE

ARGENTINA

Germany in May 1939 willing to allow Jewish refugees to leave

The voyage of the "St. Louis" May–June 1939

Countries refusing to accept refugees from the "St. Louis"

Countries accepting refugees from the "St. Louis"

© Martin Gilbert

31

THE SEARCH FOR SAFETY 1933-1945

1940 U.S. Congress rejects Bill to open Alaska to Jewish refugees

CANADA
8,000

71,000

1943 British Government rejects the appeal by the Archbishop of Canterbury to abandon the quota system

3,000

1941 U.S. tightens quota system. Congress rejects proposal to admit 20,000 German Jewish children above the quota limits

UNITED STATES
240,000

15,000

BERMUDA

1943 Secret Anglo-American conference fails to reach agreement on the possibility of an open-door policy for refugees

2,000

MEXICO

CUBA
4,500

5,000

DOMINICAN REPUBLIC

1937 Severe restrictions introduced

May 1939 Cuban and U.S. Governments refuse to admit 900 German Jewish refugees on the "St. Louis". They return to Europe.

25,000

12,000

1939-1945 Jewish immigration limited to 300 a year

7,000

14,000

50,000

January 1939 Anglo-American suggestion that Jewish refugees go to Angola not followed up for fear of offending the Portuguese

Under German occupation or control by December 1941. Home of 8 million Jews

Countries almost entirely closed to Jewish refugees

Countries restricting Jewish immigration by means of a quota system or other barriers

Countries partially, but not entirely restricting Jewish immigration

City accepting more Jewish refugees than were allowed to enter Canada, Australia, New Zealand, British Africa, South Africa and India (all in the British Empire) combined

5,000 Number of Jewish refugees allowed to enter 1933-1945. Shanghai alone required no visa

32

1943 U.S. State Department rejects Swedish proposal for joint rescue of 20,000 Jewish children from Germany

Closed to European refugees

U. S. S. R.
250,000

JEWISH AUTONOMOUS BIROBIDJAN (U.S.S.R)

90,000

CHINA
5,000

JAPAN
2,000

Shanghai
25,000

ANGOLA

8,000

.MAURITIUS
1,750

AUSTRALIA
9,000

Jews deported by the British from Palestine while seeking "illegal entry". They were allowed to enter Palestine in 1945

1933-1935 Unrestricted immigration. Then almost no Jews allowed in 1936-1945

"They that sow in tears
  Shall reap in joy.
He that goeth forth and weepeth,
  Bearing precious seed,
Shall doubtless come again with rejoicing
  Bringing his sheaves with him"

PSALM 126

© Martin Gilbert

JEWISH SETTLEMENTS AND IMMIGRATION, 1931 – 1942

- Jewish settlements established between 1931 and 1939

▮ Entry points for 'illegal' immigrants, who were landed on the open beaches, often at night

Palestine is our only anchor in these days of adversity. If the gates of Palestine are closed there is no hope left.
FRANZ KAHN TO THE ZIONIST CONGRESS, GENEVA, 22 AUGUST 1939 HIS HOMELAND, CZECHOSLOVAKIA, HAD BEEN OCCUPIED BY GERMANY IN MARCH 1939

Hanita
Nahariya
Haifa
Tiberias
Sea of Galilee
Ein Gev
Tantura
Afula
Caesaria

JEWISH IMMIGRATION	
1931	4, 075
1932	12, 553
1933	37, 337
1934	45, 267
1935	66, 472
1936	29, 595
1937	10, 629
1938	14, 675
1939	31, 195

Kfar Vitkin
Netanya
Tulkarm
Nablus
Herzliya
Tel Aviv

Mediterranean Sea

Kallia
Beit Haarava
Jerusalem
Majdal
Negba
Jibalya
Gaza
Hebron
Dead Sea
Beersheba
Sodom
Negev

0 5 10 15
Miles

Despite the Arab riots of 1929, Jewish immigration continued to grow, and Jewish settlements were founded throughout Palestine. The Arab leaders protested against this new influx of immigrants and refugees, and following a new Arab campaign in 1936, the British authorities introduced a strict limit to Jewish immigration (a maximum of 8,000 between August 1937 and March 1938). As a result of still more Arab pressure, the British published their Palestine White Paper on 17 May 1939. Only 10,643 Jews were allowed to enter in 1940, 4,592 in 1941 and 4,206 in 1942, at a time when the fierce German persecution of Jews in Europe made the need for a place of refuge a desperate one. Between July 1934 and September 1939 the Zionists disembarked 15,000 'illegal' immigrants on the Palestine coast, from a total of 43 ships. On 4 September 1939 two 'illegal' immigrants were killed when their ship was fired on by a British cutter. Later 'illegals' were deported to Cyprus and Mauritius

© Martin Gilbert

33

BRITISH RESTRICTIONS ON JEWISH LAND PURCHASE 1940

These regulations prevented the Jews from extending their land holdings in three main areas of Jewish settlement: around Jerusalem, around Beersheba, and north of Acre

Legend:

–··– Boundary of Britain's Palestine Mandate, 1922-1948

Area closed by Britain to all further Jewish land purchase after 28 February 1940 (4,104,000 acres)

Land bought by Jews between 1880 and 1940, within the area closed to all future Jewish purchase in 1940

A Areas of dense Jewish land settlements before 1940, in which Jews were to be allowed to continue to buy land

B Areas of substantial Jewish settlement before 1940, in which further Jewish purchases were to be strictly curtailed

0 5 10 15
Miles

Nahariya
Acre
Haifa
Sea of Galilee
Jenin
Beit Shean
Tulkarm
Nablus
Tel Aviv
Jaffa
Ramallah
Jericho
Ramla
Jerusalem
Bethlehem
Hebron
Gaza
Dead Sea
Khan Yunis
Rafah
Beersheba

Mediterranean Sea

The effect of these Regulations is that no Jew may acquire in Palestine a plot of land, a building, or a tree, or any right in water, except in towns and a very small part of the country. The Regulations deny to Jews equality before the law and introduce racial discrimination. They confine the Jews within a small pale of settlement similar to that which existed in Czarist Russia before the last war, and such as now exists only under Nazi rule. They not only violate the terms of the Mandate but completely nullify its primary purpose
DAVID BEN GURION
28 FEBUARY 1940

© Martin Gilbert

THE EXTERMINATION OF JEWS 1941-1945

Germany in 1937 (under Nazi rule since 1933)

Under German control or influence 1941-1944

Main German concentration camps

8,700,000 (total) Approximate Jewish populations in 1941

5,800,000 (total) Estimated number of Jews murdered by 1945. This figure is the minimum estimate, made in early 1970

© Martin Gilbert

The Germans also killed over six million non-Jewish civilians 1939-1945, in concentration camps, reprisals, bombing, and slave labour camps.

German occupied RUSSIA (1941-1944)
2,500,000
750,000

Black Sea

BESSARABIA

RUMANIA
1,000,000
750,000

BULGARIA
48,000
40,000

LATVIA
100,000
70,000

LITHUANIA
140,000
104,000

Stutthof
EAST PRUSSIA

Treblinka
Sobibor
Chelmno POLAND
Majdanek Belzec
Auschwitz

3,000,000
2,600,000

281,000
277,000

HUNGARY
710,000
402,000

YUGOSLAVIA
70,000
60,000

GREECE
67,000
65,000

ALBANIA

Ravensbrück
Sachsenhausen
Grossrosen
Neuengamme
Belsen
GERMANY
Mittelbaudora Buchenwald
Flossenberg Dachau
Theresienstadt
CZECHOSLOVAKIA
Mauthausen
AUSTRIA

250,000
180,000

70,000
65,000

ITALY
120,000
9,000

DENMARK
6,000
100

HOLLAND
140,000
106,000
Vught

BELGIUM
85,000
28,000

FRANCE
300,000
83,000

0   200
Miles

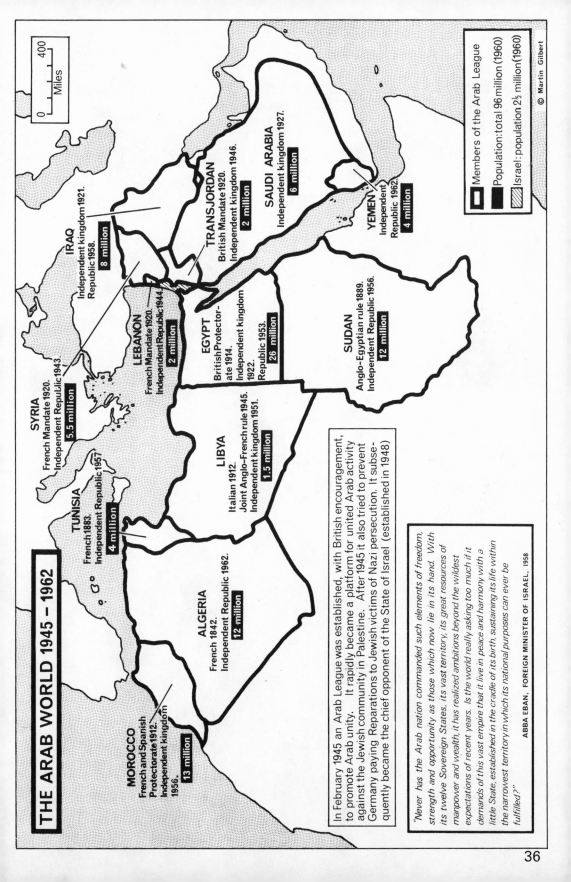

THE ARAB WORLD 1945 – 1962

MOROCCO
French and Spanish
Protectorate 1912.
Independent Kingdom
1956.
13 million

ALGERIA
French 1842.
Independent Republic 1962.
12 million

TUNISIA
French 1883.
Independent Republic 1957
4 million

LIBYA
Italian 1912.
Joint Anglo-French rule 1945.
Independent kingdom 1951.
1.5 million

SYRIA
French Mandate 1920.
Independent Republic 1943
5.5 million

LEBANON
French Mandate 1920.
Independent Republic 1944.
2 million

IRAQ
Independent kingdom 1921.
Republic 1958.
8 million

TRANSJORDAN
British Mandate 1920.
Independent kingdom 1946.
2 million

SAUDI ARABIA
Independent kingdom 1927.
6 million

YEMEN
Independent
Republic 1962.
4 million

EGYPT
British Protector-
ate 1914.
Independent kingdom
1922.
Republic 1953.
26 million

SUDAN
Anglo-Egyptian rule 1889.
Independent Republic 1956.
12 million

Miles
0   400

Members of the Arab League

Population: total 96 million (1960)

Israel: population 2½ million (1960)

© Martin Gilbert

In February 1945 an Arab League was established, with British encouragement,
to promote Arab unity.   It rapidly became a platform for united Arab activity
against the Jewish community in Palestine.   After 1945 it also tried to prevent
Germany paying Reparations to Jewish victims of Nazi persecution. It subsequently became the chief opponent of the State of Israel (established in 1948)

*"Never has the Arab nation commanded such elements of freedom,
strength and opportunity as those which now lie in its hand. With
its twelve Sovereign States, its vast territory, its great resources of
manpower and wealth, it has realized ambitions beyond the wildest
expectations of recent years. Is the world really asking too much if it
demands of this vast empire that it live in peace and harmony with a
little State, established in the cradle of its birth, sustaining its life within
the narrowest territory in which its national purposes can ever be
fulfilled?"*

ABBA EBAN, FOREIGN MINISTER OF ISRAEL, 1958

36

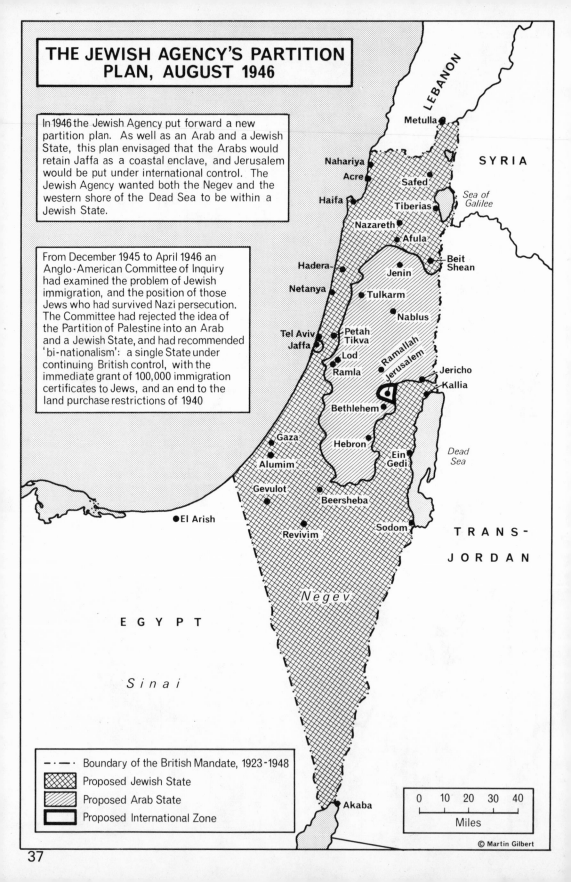

THE JEWISH AGENCY'S PARTITION PLAN, AUGUST 1946

In 1946 the Jewish Agency put forward a new partition plan. As well as an Arab and a Jewish State, this plan envisaged that the Arabs would retain Jaffa as a coastal enclave, and Jerusalem would be put under international control. The Jewish Agency wanted both the Negev and the western shore of the Dead Sea to be within a Jewish State.

From December 1945 to April 1946 an Anglo-American Committee of Inquiry had examined the problem of Jewish immigration, and the position of those Jews who had survived Nazi persecution. The Committee had rejected the idea of the Partition of Palestine into an Arab and a Jewish State, and had recommended 'bi-nationalism': a single State under continuing British control, with the immediate grant of 100,000 immigration certificates to Jews, and an end to the land purchase restrictions of 1940

LEBANON

SYRIA

Metulla

Nahariya
Acre
Safed
Sea of Galilee
Haifa
Tiberias
Nazareth
Afula
Beit Shean
Hadera
Jenin
Netanya
Tulkarm
Nablus
Tel Aviv
Jaffa
Petah Tikva
Lod
Ramallah
Ramla
Jerusalem
Jericho
Kallia
Bethlehem

Gaza
Hebron
Ein Gedi
Dead Sea
Alumim

Gevulot
Beersheba
TRANS-
●El Arish
Revivim
Sodom
JORDAN

E G Y P T

N e g e v

S i n a i

Akaba

–·– Boundary of the British Mandate, 1923-1948
Proposed Jewish State
Proposed Arab State
Proposed International Zone

0 10 20 30 40
Miles

© Martin Gilbert

37

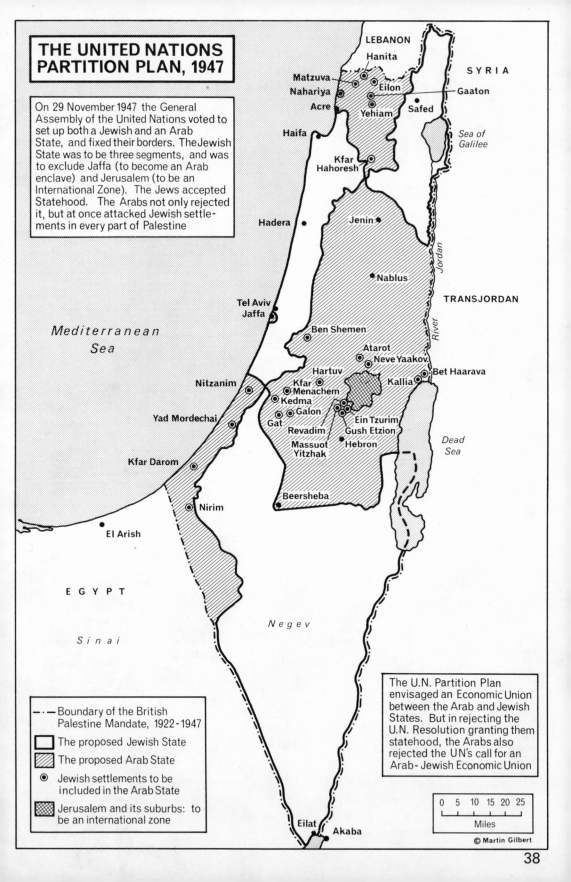

THE UNITED NATIONS PARTITION PLAN, 1947

On 29 November 1947 the General Assembly of the United Nations voted to set up both a Jewish and an Arab State, and fixed their borders. The Jewish State was to be three segments, and was to exclude Jaffa (to become an Arab enclave) and Jerusalem (to be an International Zone). The Jews accepted Statehood. The Arabs not only rejected it, but at once attacked Jewish settlements in every part of Palestine

LEBANON

SYRIA

Hanita

Matzuva

Nahariya

Eilon

Gaaton

Acre

Yehiam

Safed

Haifa

Sea of Galilee

Kfar Hahoresh

Jenin

Hadera

Nablus

TRANSJORDAN

Mediterranean Sea

Tel Aviv

Jaffa

Ben Shemen

Atarot

Neve Yaakov

Hartuv

Jordan River

Kfar Menachem

Kallia

Bet Haarava

Nitzanim

Kedma

Galon

Yad Mordechai

Gat

Revadim

Ein Tzurim

Gush Etzion

Massuot Yitzhak

Hebron

Dead Sea

Kfar Darom

Nirim

Beersheba

El Arish

EGYPT

Sinai

Negev

The U.N. Partition Plan envisaged an Economic Union between the Arab and Jewish States. But in rejecting the U.N. Resolution granting them statehood, the Arabs also rejected the UN's call for an Arab-Jewish Economic Union

— - — Boundary of the British Palestine Mandate, 1922-1947

☐ The proposed Jewish State

▨ The proposed Arab State

⊙ Jewish settlements to be included in the Arab State

▨ Jerusalem and its suburbs: to be an international zone

Eilat

Akaba

0 5 10 15 20 25
Miles

© Martin Gilbert

38

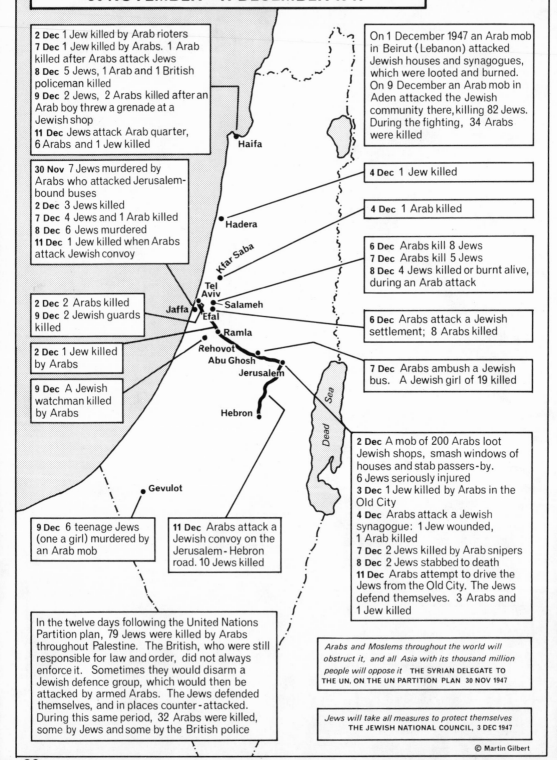

THE IMMEDIATE RESPONSE TO THE UNITED NATIONS PARTITION PLAN 30 NOVEMBER – 11 DECEMBER 1947

0   10   20
Miles

2 Dec 1 Jew killed by Arab rioters
7 Dec 1 Jew killed by Arabs. 1 Arab killed after Arabs attack Jews
8 Dec 5 Jews, 1 Arab and 1 British policeman killed
9 Dec 2 Jews, 2 Arabs killed after an Arab boy threw a grenade at a Jewish shop
11 Dec Jews attack Arab quarter, 6 Arabs and 1 Jew killed

On 1 December 1947 an Arab mob in Beirut (Lebanon) attacked Jewish houses and synagogues, which were looted and burned. On 9 December an Arab mob in Aden attacked the Jewish community there, killing 82 Jews. During the fighting, 34 Arabs were killed

Haifa

30 Nov 7 Jews murdered by Arabs who attacked Jerusalem-bound buses
2 Dec 3 Jews killed
7 Dec 4 Jews and 1 Arab killed
8 Dec 6 Jews murdered
11 Dec 1 Jew killed when Arabs attack Jewish convoy

4 Dec 1 Jew killed

4 Dec 1 Arab killed

Hadera

Kfar Saba

6 Dec Arabs kill 8 Jews
7 Dec Arabs kill 5 Jews
8 Dec 4 Jews killed or burnt alive, during an Arab attack

Tel Aviv

Jaffa   Salameh
Efal

2 Dec 2 Arabs killed
9 Dec 2 Jewish guards killed

Ramla

6 Dec Arabs attack a Jewish settlement; 8 Arabs killed

Rehovot
Abu Ghosh
Jerusalem

2 Dec 1 Jew killed by Arabs

7 Dec Arabs ambush a Jewish bus. A Jewish girl of 19 killed

9 Dec A Jewish watchman killed by Arabs

Hebron

Dead Sea

2 Dec A mob of 200 Arabs loot Jewish shops, smash windows of houses and stab passers-by. 6 Jews seriously injured
3 Dec 1 Jew killed by Arabs in the Old City
4 Dec Arabs attack a Jewish synagogue: 1 Jew wounded, 1 Arab killed
7 Dec 2 Jews killed by Arab snipers
8 Dec 2 Jews stabbed to death
11 Dec Arabs attempt to drive the Jews from the Old City. The Jews defend themselves. 3 Arabs and 1 Jew killed

Gevulot

9 Dec 6 teenage Jews (one a girl) murdered by an Arab mob

11 Dec Arabs attack a Jewish convoy on the Jerusalem-Hebron road. 10 Jews killed

In the twelve days following the United Nations Partition plan, 79 Jews were killed by Arabs throughout Palestine. The British, who were still responsible for law and order, did not always enforce it. Sometimes they would disarm a Jewish defence group, which would then be attacked by armed Arabs. The Jews defended themselves, and in places counter-attacked. During this same period, 32 Arabs were killed, some by Jews and some by the British police

Arabs and Moslems throughout the world will obstruct it, and all Asia with its thousand million people will oppose it THE SYRIAN DELEGATE TO THE UN, ON THE UN PARTITION PLAN 30 NOV 1947

Jews will take all measures to protect themselves THE JEWISH NATIONAL COUNCIL, 3 DEC 1947

© Martin Gilbert

ARAB ATTACKS AND THE JEWISH REACTION 12 - 23 DECEMBER 1947

0 5 10 15
Miles

Arab attacks on Jews continued unabated from 12 December 1947 until the end of the year. At the same time, there was an increase in the number of Jewish terrorist reprisals. The Jewish Agency opposed these reprisals, which it denounced on 13 December, as 'spectacular exploits to gratify popular feeling'; its own defence force, the Haganah confined its activities to   defending Jewish settlements and to repulsing Arab attacks

LEBANON

SYRIA

20 Dec 1 Lebanese and 1 Syrian Arab killed by Jewish terrorists

Safed

13 Dec 13 Arabs killed by Jewish terrorists. 1 Jew killed by Arabs
19 Dec 1 Jew killed by Arabs after wandering into the Arab quarter
24 Dec 4 Jews killed by Arab snipers. 4 Arabs killed as reprisals

Haifa

15 Dec 2 Arabs killed during their attack on Jewish farms

12 Dec 2 Jewish employees of British Overseas Airways, and 1 Jewish cook, killed by Arabs

13 Dec 13 Arabs killed by Jewish terrorists
22 Dec 2 Arabs killed while attacking Jewish homes

14 Dec Arabs kill 14 Jews who were taking supplies to a children's village

Kfar Saba

22 Dec 2 Jews killed by Arabs. 1 Arab killed in reprisal

Tel Aviv • Petah Tikva
Jaffa

19 Dec 1 Jew killed in Arab attack on road convoy

Holon
Lydda
Ramla
Ben Shemen

14 Dec 1 Jew and 1 Arab killed

Jerusalem

Bab-el-Wad • Silwan

12 Dec 5 Arabs killed, 47 injured at Damascus gate bus station by a Jewish terrorist bomb
13 Dec 1 Jewish child killed in Arab attack
22 Dec 1 Jew killed by Arabs. 2 British soldiers killed by Jewish terrorists as reprisal for raping a Jewish girl
23 Dec 2 Jews killed by Arabs. 1 Arab killed by Jews in self defence

13 Dec 1 Jew killed in an Arab attack

20 Dec 1 Arab killed as reprisal for repeated Arab attacks on Jewish road traffic

Gaza

Alumim

Mishmar Hanegev

Gevulot

Beersheba

18 Dec 1 Jew killed by Arabs

Halutza

13 Dec 3 Jews killed beating off an Arab attack

16 Dec 1 Jew killed in an Arab attack

12 Dec 3 Jews murdered, 4 missing after Arab attack

12 Dec 3 Jews killed by Arabs while inspecting a water pipe

© Martin Gilbert

ARAB ATTACKS AND THE JEWISH REACTION
24 - 31 DECEMBER 1947

In the twenty days between the 12th and 31st December, one hundred and twenty six Jews were killed by Arabs. More than 30 Arabs were killed while attacking Jewish settlements, and over 60 Arabs were killed as reprisals by terrorists

24 Dec 4 Jews killed by Arab snipers; 4 Arabs killed in counterattack
27 Dec 2 Jews killed by Arabs. 1 Arab killed in counterattack
30 Dec 6 Arabs killed by a Jewish terrorist bomb. Thirty-nine Jewish workmen killed by Arabs as a reprisal
31 Dec 1 Jew shot dead by an Arab sniper

30 Dec 2 Jews killed by an Arab mob

Safed

25 Dec 10 Arabs and 2 Jews killed in battle between Arabs and Jews

Haifa
Hadar Hacarmel

27 Dec 1 Jew killed by Arabs

24 Dec 1 Jewish watchman killed by Arabs

Tel Mond

26 Dec 7 Jews killed by Arabs while driving in convoy to Jerusalem

Tel Aviv

Jaffa

27 Dec 2 Jews killed during an Arab attack on a Jewish convoy

Bab-el-Wad

Jerusalem

Beit Safafa

28 Dec 5 Jews killed by Arab snipers. 5 Arabs killed by Jewish terrorists in reprisal
29 Dec 13 Arabs killed by Jewish terrorists. 2 Jews killed by Arabs
30 Dec Arabs murder a Jewish passer-by on Mount Zion. 1 Jew, 1 British policeman killed during a Jewish funeral on Mount of Olives
31 Dec 3 Jews killed during Arab attack on a bus. 2 Jews murdered by Arabs in individual attacks

Gaza

Beersheba

Hatzerim

25 Dec 2 Jewish guards killed by Arabs
27 Dec 1 Jew killed in an Arab attack 1 Arab killed when attack beaten off
28 Dec 1 Arab killed during attack on Jews
29 Dec 3 Jews killed by Arab mortar fire. 1 Jew killed by Arab snipers

24 Dec 3 Arabs killed by Jews while trying to damage a water pipeline

25 Dec 1 Arab killed when Jews reply to Arab sniper fire

© Martin Gilbert

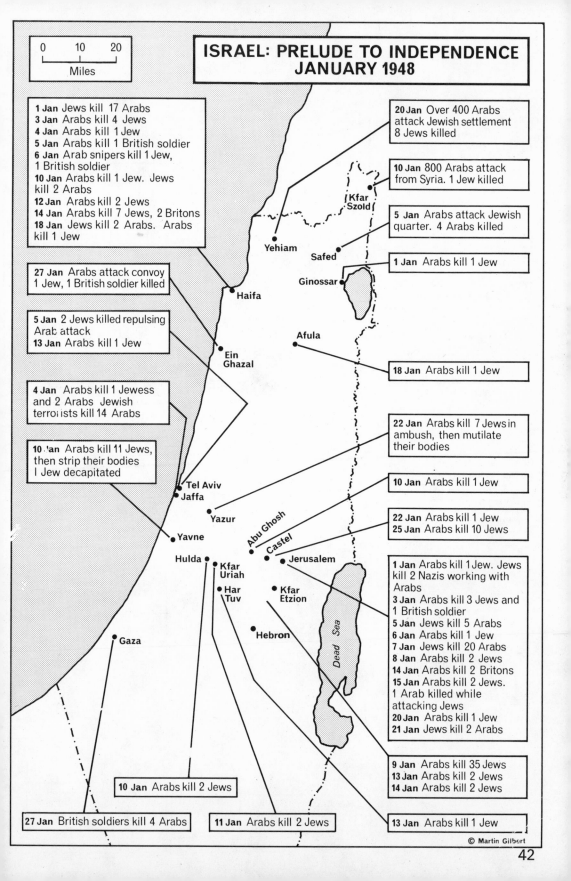

ISRAEL: PRELUDE TO INDEPENDENCE JANUARY 1948

0 10 20 Miles

1 Jan Jews kill 17 Arabs
3 Jan Arabs kill 4 Jews
4 Jan Arabs kill 1 Jew
5 Jan Arabs kill 1 British soldier
6 Jan Arab snipers kill 1 Jew, 1 British soldier
10 Jan Arabs kill 1 Jew. Jews kill 2 Arabs
12 Jan Arabs kill 2 Jews
14 Jan Arabs kill 7 Jews, 2 Britons
18 Jan Jews kill 2 Arabs. Arabs kill 1 Jew

27 Jan Arabs attack convoy 1 Jew, 1 British soldier killed

5 Jan 2 Jews killed repulsing Arab attack
13 Jan Arabs kill 1 Jew

4 Jan Arabs kill 1 Jewess and 2 Arabs Jewish terrorists kill 14 Arabs

10 Jan Arabs kill 11 Jews, then strip their bodies 1 Jew decapitated

20 Jan Over 400 Arabs attack Jewish settlement 8 Jews killed

10 Jan 800 Arabs attack from Syria. 1 Jew killed

5 Jan Arabs attack Jewish quarter. 4 Arabs killed

1 Jan Arabs kill 1 Jew

18 Jan Arabs kill 1 Jew

22 Jan Arabs kill 7 Jews in ambush, then mutilate their bodies

10 Jan Arabs kill 1 Jew

22 Jan Arabs kill 1 Jew
25 Jan Arabs kill 10 Jews

1 Jan Arabs kill 1 Jew. Jews kill 2 Nazis working with Arabs
3 Jan Arabs kill 3 Jews and 1 British soldier
5 Jan Jews kill 5 Arabs
6 Jan Arabs kill 1 Jew
7 Jan Jews kill 20 Arabs
8 Jan Arabs kill 2 Jews
14 Jan Arabs kill 2 Britons
15 Jan Arabs kill 2 Jews. 1 Arab killed while attacking Jews
20 Jan Arabs kill 1 Jew
21 Jan Jews kill 2 Arabs

9 Jan Arabs kill 35 Jews
13 Jan Arabs kill 2 Jews
14 Jan Arabs kill 2 Jews

10 Jan Arabs kill 2 Jews

27 Jan British soldiers kill 4 Arabs

11 Jan Arabs kill 2 Jews

13 Jan Arabs kill 1 Jew

Kfar Szold
Yehiam
Safed
Ginossar
Haifa
Afula
Ein Ghazal
Tel Aviv
Jaffa
Yazur
Abu Ghosh
Castel
Yavne
Hulda
Kfar Uriah
Jerusalem
Har Tuv
Kfar Etzion
Gaza
Hebron
Dead Sea

© Martin Gilbert

42

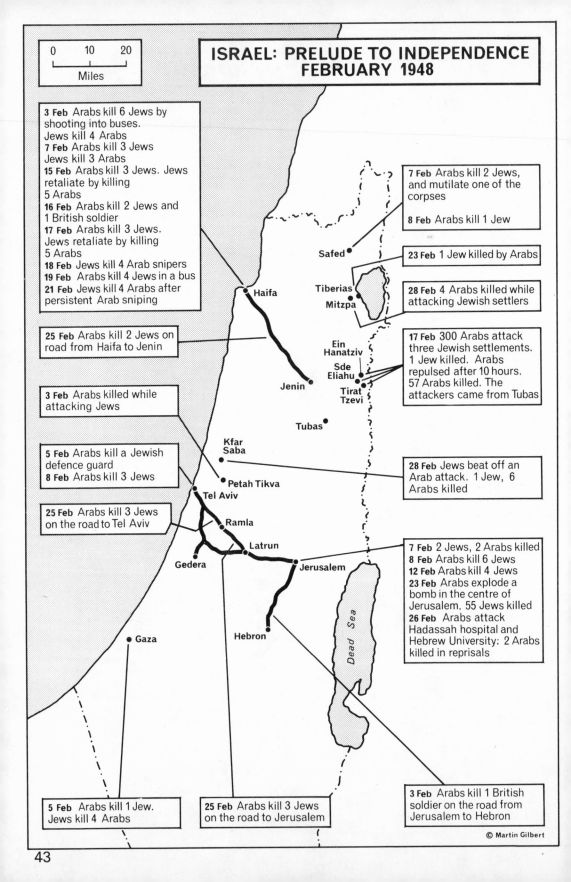

ISRAEL: PRELUDE TO INDEPENDENCE FEBRUARY 1948

0   10   20
Miles

3 Feb Arabs kill 6 Jews by shooting into buses.
Jews kill 4 Arabs
7 Feb Arabs kill 3 Jews
Jews kill 3 Arabs
15 Feb Arabs kill 3 Jews. Jews retaliate by killing
5 Arabs
16 Feb Arabs kill 2 Jews and 1 British soldier
17 Feb Arabs kill 3 Jews. Jews retaliate by killing
5 Arabs
18 Feb Jews kill 4 Arab snipers
19 Feb Arabs kill 4 Jews in a bus
21 Feb Jews kill 4 Arabs after persistent Arab sniping

25 Feb Arabs kill 2 Jews on road from Haifa to Jenin

3 Feb Arabs killed while attacking Jews

5 Feb Arabs kill a Jewish defence guard
8 Feb Arabs kill 3 Jews

25 Feb Arabs kill 3 Jews on the road to Tel Aviv

7 Feb Arabs kill 2 Jews, and mutilate one of the corpses
8 Feb Arabs kill 1 Jew

23 Feb 1 Jew killed by Arabs

28 Feb 4 Arabs killed while attacking Jewish settlers

17 Feb 300 Arabs attack three Jewish settlements. 1 Jew killed. Arabs repulsed after 10 hours. 57 Arabs killed. The attackers came from Tubas

28 Feb Jews beat off an Arab attack. 1 Jew, 6 Arabs killed

7 Feb 2 Jews, 2 Arabs killed
8 Feb Arabs kill 6 Jews
12 Feb Arabs kill 4 Jews
23 Feb Arabs explode a bomb in the centre of Jerusalem. 55 Jews killed
26 Feb Arabs attack Hadassah hospital and Hebrew University: 2 Arabs killed in reprisals

5 Feb Arabs kill 1 Jew. Jews kill 4 Arabs

25 Feb Arabs kill 3 Jews on the road to Jerusalem

3 Feb Arabs kill 1 British soldier on the road from Jerusalem to Hebron

Safed
Tiberias
Mitzpa
Haifa
Ein Hanatziv
Sde Eliahu
Jenin
Tirat Tzevi
Tubas
Kfar Saba
Petah Tikva
Tel Aviv
Ramla
Latrun
Gedera
Jerusalem
Gaza
Hebron
Dead Sea

© Martin Gilbert

43

ISRAEL: PRELUDE TO INDEPENDENCE MARCH 1948

0 10 20
Miles

18 March Arabs kill 4 Jews and 5 British soldiers in an attack on a convoy

Fighting between Arabs and Jews was intense throughout March. Arabs attacked Jewish transport almost daily, and Jewish reprisals were intense. During the month some 20 Jews and over 100 Arabs were killed in the Haifa area

20 March Arabs kill 7 Jews

31 March Jewish terrorists blow up train, kill 40 Arabs

4 March 1 Jewish worker killed by an Arab mine

24 March 6 Arabs killed in Jewish reprisals in which 30 more Arabs were killed in other areas

4 March Arabs mortar shell kills Jewish schoolboy
17 March Arab snipers kill a Jewish woman
29 March Arabs kill 2 Jews

1 March 28 British soldiers killed by a Jewish terrorist bomb under a train
28 March Arabs attack a Jewish convoy; 6 Arabs killed

9 March 3 Arabs killed while attacking Jewish settlement

11 March 2 Jewish farmers killed by an Arab mine
13 March Jews kill 20 Arabs in reprisals

21 March 6 Jews killed in a bus to Safed

28 March Arabs attack a Jewish convoy. 6 Arabs killed

11 March 1 Jew, 4 Arabs killed in street fighting
14 March 1 Jewish girl and 4 Arabs killed

18 March The bodies of 7 Jews found
23 March Arabs murder Jewish settler

1 March 4 Jews killed by Arabs
2 March 3 Jews killed in an Arab attack. 10 Arabs killed during the battle.
4 March Arabs kill 1 Jew

4 March Sixteen Jews, outnumbered ten to one, killed by Arabs in an ambush

Throughout March the Arabs tried to cut the roads to Jerusalem, and to kill all Jews trying to leave or enter the city. The Arabs also attack the Jewish settlements around the city, and on 11 March, planted a bomb at the Jewish Agency in the centre of the city, killing 13 Jews. The Jews defended themselves, and Jewish terrorists also took fierce reprisals. During the month over 70 Jews and 230 Arabs were killed in the Jerusalem area

26 March Arabs attack Jewish convoy 2 Jews, 6 Arabs killed

22 March 200 Arabs attack Jewish settlement. 20 Arabs 4 Jews killed

14 March 7 Jews killed by Arabs in a road ambush

Place names: Hulata, Rosh Pina, Yehiam, Safed, Acre, Haifa, Tiberias, Ein Harod, Afula, Binyamina, Hadera, Tulkarm, Tel Aviv, Rehovot, Ramallah, Atarot, Faluja, Jerusalem, Nitzanim, Gaza, Hebron, Dead Sea

© Martin Gilbert

44

BIDDU, BEIR SURIK

19 April Hagannah destroy 100 houses and kill many Iraqis at these bases for attacks on the Jerusalem-Tel Aviv road

CASTEL

end March Occupied by Syrian Iraqi troops
2 April Occupied by the Hagan 1 Jew killed
6 April 3 Jews killed
7 April 7 Arabs killed
8 April Arab Commander kille
11 April Jews destroy Arab vill of Kolonia, from which Castel attacks had been launched. The inhabitants had already b evacuated

Mediterranean Sea

Tel Aviv

Jaffa

Beit Dagan

Ben Shemen

Lydda

Rishon le Zion

Ramla

ROAD USED TO REACH JERUSALEM AFTER ARABS CUT RAMLA SECTION OF MAIN ROAD

Rehovot

MAIN ROAD TEL AVIV TO JERUSALEM

Latrun

Deir Ayub

Hulda

THE 'BURMA ROAD' BUILT AFTER ARABS CUT DEIR AYUB SECTION OF MAIN ROAD

RAMLA

12 April Hagannah blow up 12 buildings in area from which Jerusalem road attacks had come

In the six weeks before the British withdrew from Palestine, the Arabs did everything in their power to prevent the Jews from reaching Jerusalem, and sought to disrupt all Jewish life within the city. Many of the Arabs involved were regular soldiers from Syria and Iraq

 Constant Arab sniping throughout April and May 1948 against vehicles on the roads to Jerusalem

LYDDA

5 April Hagannah kill 10 Iraqi soldiers in camp from which the Jerusalam road had been under attack

DEIR AYUB

20 April 6 Jews killed in an Arab ambush

DEIR YASSIN

9 April Jewish terrorists massacre over 200 Arabs. The Jewish Agency and the Hagannah both immediately condemned the killings as 'utterly repugnant'

SARIS

16 April Jews capture Syrian arm base. Several dozen Syrians, a 3 Jews killed

KFAR ETZION

13 April Attack by 400 troops repulsed
20-30 April Jews repel repeated Arab attacks
4 May Arab attacks beaten off; 12 Arabs killed
12 May Several hundred Arabs renew the attack. 100 Jews kill Only 4 survive. 15 Jews were machine gunned to death after t had surrendered, and were bein photographed by their captors

© Martin Gilbert

45

THE BATTLE FOR THE JERUSALEM ROADS
1 APRIL – 14 MAY 1948

NEBI SAMUEL
24 April Jews attack base of Arab raids on both the Ramallah and Tel Aviv roads. 25 Jews, 6 Arabs killed

NEVE YAAKOV
18 April 1 Jew killed in heavy Arab attack on settlement
19 April Jews attack Shuafat base for the attack on Neve Yaakov

SHEIKH JARRAH
13 April Arabs attack a convoy of Jewish doctors and nurses on their way to the Hadassah hospital on Mount Scopus. Many were shot as they ran from their burning vehicles. 40 Jews killed

TRANS-JORDAN

River Jordan

Ramallah

Jericho

Bet Haarava

Ataroth

Nebi Samuel

Neve Yaakov

Kallia

Biddu

ir Surik

Kolonia

Shuafat

Sheikh Jarrah

Saris

Castel

Motza

Deir Yassin

Mount Scopus

JERUSALEM

Talpioth

Ein Feshha

Battir

Ramat Rachel

Beit Jalla

Bethlehem

JERUSALEM
1 April Arabs attack Jews: 17 Arabs killed when attack repulsed
2 April Arabs kill 1 Jew
4 April Arabs kill 1 Jew
6 April Arabs kill 1 Jew
7 April Arabs kill 2 Jews
9 April Arab mortar fire kills a 12 year old Jewish girl
17 April 1 Jew killed in Arab mortar fire
18 April Arab snipers kill a Jewess. 3 Arab snipers killed
22 April Arab snipers kill 2 Jews
24 April Arabs kill 3 Jews
25 April Arab mortar fire kills 1 Jew 45 Arabs killed in counterattack

Revadim

Massuat Yitzhak

Ein Tzurim

Kfar Etzion

D e a d   S e a

EIN TZURIM
14 May The last settlement of the Etzion block captured by the Arabs Its survivors watched their settlement being plundered

1 2 3
Miles

Hebron

ISRAEL: PRELUDE TO INDEPENDENCE 1 APRIL – 14 MAY 1948

LEBANON

SYRIA

Damascus •

At the beginning of April, spasmodic fighting ended, and Arab military units from Syria, Iraq, and Egypt increased their efforts to drive the Jews from the Galilee and the Negev. The Jews defended their settlements with tenacity. As the British withdrew from the towns, the Arabs and Jews fought to control them. The Jews took over Tiberias (19 April), Haifa (23 April), Acre (26 April), Safed (11 May) and Jaffa (12 May)

10 May Jews repulse three thousand Syrian and Iraqi troops in house-to-house fighting

Dan
Daphne
Lehavot Habashan
Ramot Naftali

Nahariya
Acre
Safed

GALILEE

The Jewish attack was a direct consequence of continuous attacks by Arabs on Jews in Haifa over the previous four days. The attack was carried out by the Haganah and there was no massacre.
THE BRITISH HIGH COMMISSIONER 24 APRIL 1948

Haifa
Tiberias
Sea of Galilee
Degania
Afula
Gesher

Mishmar Haemek

Beit Alpha
Tirat Tzevi

19 April After an attack by Arabs from the surrounding areas, the Jews occupied the Arab quarters of the town, and at the same time declared: *the day will come when the Arabs will return to their homes and prosperity in this town. In the meantime, let no citizens dare to lay hands on Arab property.*

I do not mind the destruction of Jaffa if we can achieve the destruction of Tel Aviv.
THE IRAQI OFFICER COMMANDING ARAB TROOPS IN JAFFA, APRIL 1948

Kfar Saba
Petah Tikva
Jaffa
Tel Aviv
Rishon-le-Zion
Lydda
Ramalla
Rehovot
Latrun
Gedera
Jerusalem
Nitzanim
Kfar Etzion

• Amman

TRANSJORDAN

The choice for our people, Mr President, is between statehood and extermination. **DR. WEIZMANN TO PRESIDENT TRUMAN 9 APRIL 1948**

Mediterranean Sea

Gaza
Dorot
Rumana
Kfar Darom
Alumim
Shoval
Nirim
Mishmar Hanegev
Gevulot
Nevatim

Hebron

Dead Sea

N e g e v
Halutza
Revivim

EGYPT

From mid-April, Arabs began to leave their villages in large numbers, encouraged to flee by their leaders. By the end of April over 20,000 Arabs had crossed into Lebanon and Syria. By 5 May over 65,000 Arabs had left Haifa and over 50,000 had left Jaffa

Do not fear. Do not destroy your homes with your own hands. Do not block off your sources of livelihood. Do not bring tragedy upon yourselves by unnecessary evacuation and self-imposed burdens. By moving out you will be overtaken by poverty and humiliation.
APPEAL TO HAIFA'S ARABS BY THE FEDERATION OF JEWISH WORKERS 28.4.1948

0 5 10 15
Miles

//// Areas of principal Arab attacks April–May 1948

▦ Areas of principal Jewish counterattacks, leading to Jewish control of Haifa, Acre, Jaffa, Safed and Tiberias

═ Roads under continual Arab siege, kept open by the Jews only by continual fighting, and with heavy loss of life

© Martin Gilbert

THE ARAB INVASION OF THE STATE OF ISRAEL 15 MAY 1948

Principal Arab attacks from outside Palestine

Territory allocated to the State of Israel by the United Nations, but overrun by the Arabs between 15 May and 1 June 1948

Territory remaining under Israeli control on 1 June 1948

Jewish settlements overrun by the Arabs between 15 May and 1 June, often after fierce resistance

Jewish settlements surrounded by Arab forces, but resisting repeated attempts to overrun them between 15 May and 1 June, despite grave shortages of arms and men

On 15 May 1948 six Arab armies, those of Egypt, Syria, Transjordan, Lebanon, Saudi Arabia and Iraq invaded Israel. They advanced rapidly, threatening to destroy the one-day-old State, and drive its citizens into the sea. The Israelis resisted, and after ten days were able to counter-attack. A truce was signed on 11 June 1948

LEBANON

SYRIA

Malkiya
Kadesh

Nahariya
Acre
Haifa

Mishmar Hayarden

Ein Gev

Afula
Gesher

Degania
Naharayim

IRAQI TROOPS

Hadera

Herzliya
Tel Aviv
Jaffa

Nablus

Ben Shemen

TRANSJORDAN

Ataroт
Neve Yaakov
Mt Scopus
The Jewish Quarter:
Old City of Jerusalem

Bet Haarava

Kallia

Nitzanim

Kfar Menachem   Hartuv
Kedma   Massuot   Revadim
Yizhak
Gat   Galon   Ein Tzurim
Gush Etzion

Yad Mordechai

Kfar Darom

Nirim

Beersheba

Nevatim

Sodom

EGYPT

Sinai

Negev

Dead Sea

River Jordan

0   10   20
Miles

© Martin Gilbert

THE ISRAELI WAR OF INDEPENDENCE, 1948-1949

0 5 10 15
Miles

Between May 1948 and January 1949, the State of Israel fought to retain its independence against the combined forces of six Arab armies. Following the initial Arab invasion, the Israelis reopened the road to Jerusalem, won control of the Coastal Plain, secured the upper Galilee, and drove the Egyptians from the Negev. But the Israelis were themselves driven from the Jewish quarter of the Old City of Jerusalem (whose synagogues were desecrated and whose Jewish houses were destroyed)

During Israel's struggle for independence between November 1947 and January 1949, more than 4,000 Jewish soldiers and 2,000 civilians were killed out of a total Jewish population of only 650,000. The figures for Arab dead were not disclosed by the Arab States

LEBANON

SYRIA

Nahariya

Haifa

Ein Gev

Beit Shean

Mediterranean

Jenin

Netanya

Tulkarm

Kalkiliya

THE WEST BANK

River Jordan

TRANSJORDAN

Tel Aviv
Jaffa

Sea

Jerusalem

Amman

Gaza

Hebron

Rafah

Dead Sea

El Arish

E G Y P T

Sinai

Abu Aweigila

Kusseima

N e g e v

The regular forces of the neighbouring countries - with their equipment and their armaments - enjoy superiority at this time. However, evaluation of the possibilities cannot be merely a military consideration of arms against arms and units against units, since we do not have those arms or that armoured force. The problem is to what extent our men will be able to overcome enemy forces by virtue of their fighting spirit, of our planning and our tactics. YIGAEL YADIN, 21 MAY 1948
CHIEF OF OPERATIONS, ISRAELI ARMY

Kuntilla

Taba   Akaba

■ Under the control of the new State of Israel by 1 June 1948

▨ Conquered by Israeli forces between June and November 1948

▧ Conquered by Israeli forces between November 1948 and January 1949

--- Territory occupied by Israeli forces from which they withdrew during the early months of 1949

•—•— Frontiers of the State of Israel 1949 - 1967

© Martin Gilbert

THE ARAB REFUGEES, 1948

Main areas from which Arabs fled, April – December 1948

Towns with large Arab populations, most of whom fled

Percentage of refugees reaching new areas

000 United Nations estimate of the number of refugees reaching new areas

LEBANON
14%
100,000

IRAQ
0·6%
4,000

SYRIA
10%
75,000

Safed

Acre

Haifa

Tiberias

Mediterranean Sea

Beisan

THE WEST BANK
38%
280,000

River Jordan

TRANSJORDAN
10%
70,000

Jaffa

Ramla

THE GAZA STRIP
26%
190,000

Dead Sea

Beersheba

0   10   20
Miles

EGYPT
1%
7,000

The United Nations Partition Plan envisaged an Arab as well as a Jewish State. Most Arab refugees fled to the areas of the potential Arab State. But one of these areas, the Gaza Strip, was occupied by Egypt in 1948.   Another, the West Bank, was occupied by Transjordan in 1948, and annexed in 1950

The United Nations estimated that over 725,000 Arabs fled from Palestine between April and December 1948. The Israelis estimated that between 550,000 and 600,000 Arabs fled. Many Arabs were encouraged to leave by their own political leaders, who promised them that they would soon be able to return to their homes, once Israel had been destroyed. But over 160,000 Arabs either remained in Israel or returned to their homes in Israel during 1949

© Martin Gilbert

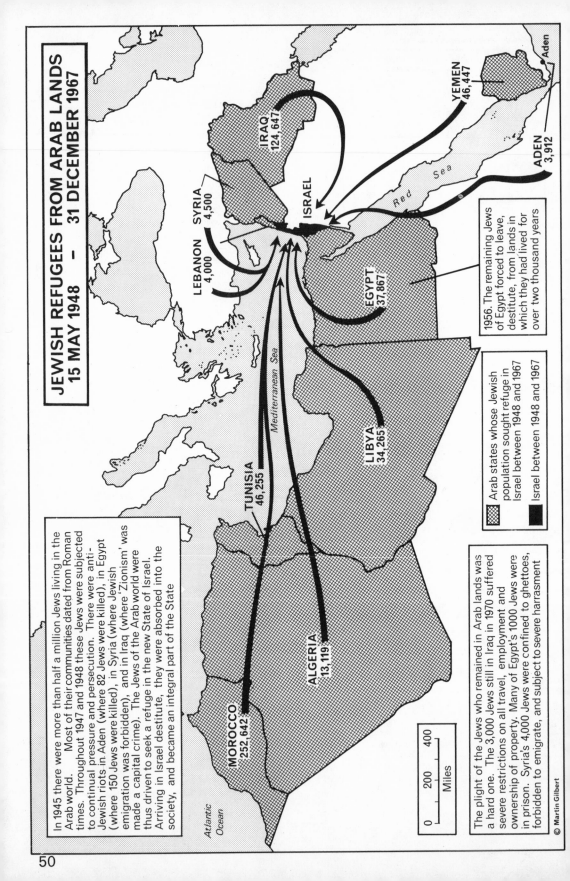

JEWISH REFUGEES FROM ARAB LANDS
15 MAY 1948 — 31 DECEMBER 1967

In 1945 there were more than half a million Jews living in the Arab world. Most of their communities dated from Roman times. Throughout 1947 and 1948 these Jews were subjected to continual pressure and persecution. There were anti-Jewish riots in Aden (where 82 Jews were killed), in Egypt (where 150 Jews were killed), in Syria (where Jewish emigration was forbidden), and in Iraq (where 'Zionism' was made a capital crime). The Jews of the Arab world were thus driven to seek a refuge in the new State of Israel. Arriving in Israel destitute, they were absorbed into the society, and became an integral part of the State

IRAQ 124,647

YEMEN 46,447

ADEN 3,912

SYRIA 4,500

LEBANON 4,000

ISRAEL

EGYPT 37,867

Red Sea

Aden

1956. The remaining Jews of Egypt forced to leave, destitute, from lands in which they had lived for over two thousand years

Mediterranean Sea

LIBYA 34,265

TUNISIA 46,255

ALGERIA 13,119

MOROCCO 252,642

Atlantic Ocean

Arab states whose Jewish population sought refuge in Israel between 1948 and 1967

Israel between 1948 and 1967

The plight of the Jews who remained in Arab lands was a hard one. The 3,000 Jews still in Iraq in 1970 suffered severe restrictions on all travel, employment and ownership of property. Many of Egypt's 1000 Jews were in prison. Syria's 4,000 Jews were confined to ghettoes, forbidden to emigrate, and subject to severe harrasment

0   200   400
Miles

© Martin Gilbert

50

JEWISH REFUGEES AND IMMIGRANTS FROM EUROPE, 15 MAY 1948 – 31 DECEMBER 1970

Between 1948 and 1970 nearly 600,000 Jews reached Israel from Europe. The majority of these were victims of Nazi persecution, whose homes and families had been destroyed. A further 60,000 Jews reached Israel from Iran and 20,000 from India. Between 1971 and 1973 over 100,000 more Soviet Jews also reached Israel

Central Europe, communist since 1948, birthplace of over 80% of the European Jewish immigrants seeking a new home and a refuge in Israel between 1948 and 1970. These Central European immigrants accounted for 36% of all Jewish immigrants to Israel during this period

Israel, borders from 1948 to 1967

SOVIET UNION

21,391

229,779

48,642

TURKEY
58,288

3,722

24,255

156,011

20,572

RUMANIA

BULGARIA

GREECE

8,063

880

3,451

3 603

POLAND

CZECHOSLOVAKIA

HUNGARY

YUGOSLAVIA

3,619

SWEDEN

AUSTRIA

4,120

ISRAEL

ITALY

11,552

GERMANY

1,899

SWITZ.

26,295

BELGIUM

HOLLAND

567

GREAT BRITAIN

FRANCE

14,006

SPAIN

0 100 200
Miles

Between 1948 and 1973 the population of Israel rose from 657,000 to over three million, an increase largely accounted for by the continual immigration

© Martin Gilbert

51

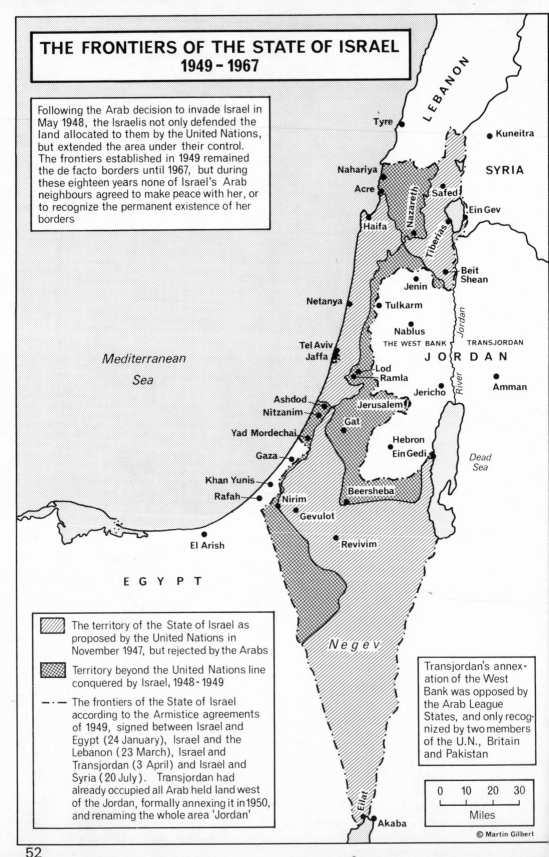

THE FRONTIERS OF THE STATE OF ISRAEL
1949 – 1967

Following the Arab decision to invade Israel in
May 1948, the Israelis not only defended the
land allocated to them by the United Nations,
but extended the area under their control.
The frontiers established in 1949 remained
the de facto borders until 1967, but during
these eighteen years none of Israel's Arab
neighbours agreed to make peace with her, or
to recognize the permanent existence of her
borders

LEBANON

SYRIA

Tyre

Kuneitra

Nahariya

Acre

Safed

Ein Gev

Haifa

Nazareth

Tiberias

Beit
Shean

Jenin

Netanya

Tulkarm

Nablus

THE WEST BANK

TRANSJORDAN

Tel Aviv
Jaffa

JORDAN

Lod
Ramla

Jordan River

Amman

Mediterranean

Sea

Ashdod
Nitzanim

Jerusalem

Jericho

Gat

Yad Mordechai

Hebron
Ein Gedi

Dead
Sea

Gaza

Khan Yunis

Beersheba

Rafah

Nirim

Gevulot

El Arish

Revivim

EGYPT

Negev

The territory of the State of Israel as
proposed by the United Nations in
November 1947, but rejected by the Arabs

Territory beyond the United Nations line
conquered by Israel, 1948-1949

—·— The frontiers of the State of Israel
according to the Armistice agreements
of 1949, signed between Israel and
Egypt (24 January), Israel and the
Lebanon (23 March), Israel and
Transjordan (3 April) and Israel and
Syria (20 July). Transjordan had
already occupied all Arab held land west
of the Jordan, formally annexing it in 1950,
and renaming the whole area 'Jordan'

Transjordan's annex-
ation of the West
Bank was opposed by
the Arab League
States, and only recog-
nized by two members
of the U.N., Britain
and Pakistan

Eilat

Akaba

0 10 20 30

Miles

© Martin Gilbert

From 1949 to 1967 Jordan refused access to Israeli's wishing to visit Old Jerusalem. In June 1967 Israel occupied the Old City, destroyed the partition barriers, and established an Israeli administration for the whole city

JERUSALEM: DIVIDED CITY 1948-1967

War Cemetery

Hadassah Medical Centre

ISRAEL

Mount Scopus

Hebrew University and National Library

MAHANAYIM

ROMEMA

SHEIKH JARRAH

GEULA

Strauss Health Centre

Mandelbaum Gate

AMERICAN COLONY

■ Tombs of the Kings

Hospital ▶

■ St George's Cathedral

Herods Gate

Hadassah Headquarters ▶

■ Rockefeller Museum

Bezalel Museum ■

MUSLIM QUARTER

St. Stephen's Gate

Mount of Olives

CHRISTIAN QUARTER

Gethsemane

Wailing Wall

Ratisbon Monastery

Yeshurun Synagogue

New Gate

■ The Holy Sepulchre

MORIA

● Dome of the Rock

■ Absalom's Tomb

ISRAEL

David's Tower

■ El Aksa Mosque

REHAVIA

ARMENIAN QUARTER

Hurva Synagogue

JORDAN

Greek Monastery ■

King David's Tomb

JEWISH QUARTER

Dung Gate

TALBIYEH

Mount Zion

■ Railway Station

GERMAN COLONY

KATAMON

GREEK COLONY

BAQAA

TALPIOTH

JORDAN

BEIT SAFAFA

0	500

Yards

━━ Western armistice-line
── Eastern armistice-line
� No Man's Land, 1948-67
▨ Built-up areas in 1948
■─ Important buildings
┼┼┼ Railway to Tel Aviv
〜〜〜 Wall of the Old City

© Martin Gilbert

53

ISRAEL'S SENSE OF INSECURITY
1949 – 1967

LEBANON

SYRIA

— · — Israel's borders 1949 - 1967

Egyptian and Syrian artillery range from the 1949 cease fire lines (20 miles range)

Egyptian and Syrian missile range from the 1949 cease fire lines (50 miles range)

Mediterranean Sea

Safed

Ein Gev

Haifa

Tiberias

Afula

Hadera

0   10   20   30

Miles

Nablus

Tel Aviv

J   O   R   D   A   N

Jerusalem

Ashkelon

Dead Sea

Gaza

Rafah   Nirim

Beersheba

Yeroham

Kusseima

N e g e v

E G Y P T

Kuntilla

'The Arab national aim is the elimination of Israel'
PRESIDENT NASSER OF EGYPT TO PRESIDENT AREF OF IRAQ, 25 MAY 1965

Between 1949 and 1967 the Arab leaders in Syria and Egypt repeatedly refused to make peace with Israel, or to accept her as a sovereign state. This refusal of the Arab states to accept even the existence of Israel was accompanied by the encouragement of continual terrorist attacks on Israeli civilians and by a series of bellicose statements

Eilat

Taba

© Martin Gilbert

CENTRAL ISRAEL AND THE JORDAN BORDER
1949–1967

0 1 2 3 4 5
Miles

−·−·− The cease-fire line between
Israel and Jordan, 1949-1967

Principal built-up areas

Distances across Israel from
the Jordanian border to the sea

Between 1949 and 1967 the whole of central Israel, from Hadera to Rehovot, lay in a narrow belt of land sandwiched between Jordan and the sea. At its most narrow, Israel was only nine miles wide, and all Israeli territory shown on this map was within Jordanian artillery range. In view of Arab threats in 1948 to cut Israel's territory in half and make the State unviable, this geographic situation constituted a permanent danger to the State of Israel

Mediterranean Sea

Jenin

Hadera

Michmoret   11 miles   **Zeita**

Netanya   **Shuweika**

Nitzanei
Oz   **Tulkarm**

10 miles

Tel Mond   **Falama**   **Nablus**

9 miles   **Kalkilya**   **J O R D A N**

Kfar   **Habla**
Saba
Herzliya

I S R A E L

*We believe that the evil which
was placed in the heart of the Arab
world should be eradicated.*
**PRESIDENT NASSER OF EGYPT TO KING
HUSSEIN OF JORDAN, 13 MARCH 1961**

Tel Aviv   **Petah
Tikva**

Jaffa   **Deir Ballut**

15 miles   **Kibya**

**Rishon
le Zion**   **Lod**   **Nilin**

Ramla   **Ramallah**

Rehovot   **Beit Sira**

18 miles   **Beit Nuba**

Latrun

© Martin Gilbert

55

THE ARAB REFUGEES 1949-1967

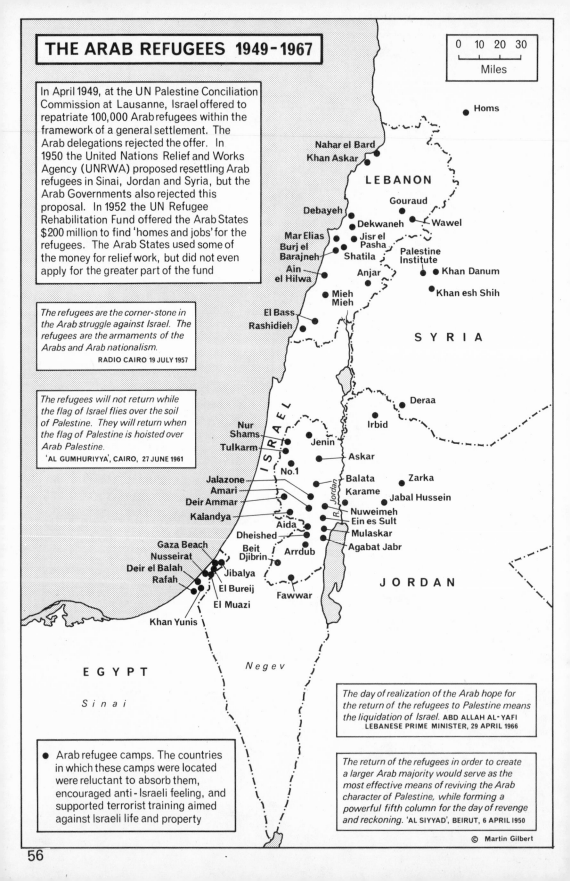

In April 1949, at the UN Palestine Conciliation Commission at Lausanne, Israel offered to repatriate 100,000 Arab refugees within the framework of a general settlement. The Arab delegations rejected the offer. In 1950 the United Nations Relief and Works Agency (UNRWA) proposed resettling Arab refugees in Sinai, Jordan and Syria, but the Arab Governments also rejected this proposal. In 1952 the UN Refugee Rehabilitation Fund offered the Arab States $200 million to find 'homes and jobs' for the refugees. The Arab States used some of the money for relief work, but did not even apply for the greater part of the fund

The refugees are the corner-stone in the Arab struggle against Israel. The refugees are the armaments of the Arabs and Arab nationalism.
RADIO CAIRO 19 JULY 1957

The refugees will not return while the flag of Israel flies over the soil of Palestine. They will return when the flag of Palestine is hoisted over Arab Palestine.
'AL GUMHURIYYA', CAIRO, 27 JUNE 1961

The day of realization of the Arab hope for the return of the refugees to Palestine means the liquidation of Israel. **ABD ALLAH AL-YAFI LEBANESE PRIME MINISTER, 29 APRIL 1966**

The return of the refugees in order to create a larger Arab majority would serve as the most effective means of reviving the Arab character of Palestine, while forming a powerful fifth column for the day of revenge and reckoning. **'AL SIYYAD', BEIRUT, 6 APRIL 1950**

● Arab refugee camps. The countries in which these camps were located were reluctant to absorb them, encouraged anti-Israeli feeling, and supported terrorist training aimed against Israeli life and property

0 10 20 30
Miles

Homs

Nahar el Bard
Khan Askar

LEBANON

Gouraud
Debayeh
Dekwaneh   Wawel
Mar Elias   Jisr el
Burj el   Pasha   Palestine
Barajneh   Shatila   Institute
Ain   Khan Danum
el Hilwa   Anjar
                       Khan esh Shih
Mieh
Mieh

El Bass
Rashidieh   **SYRIA**

                  Deraa

         Irbid
Nur
Shams   Jenin
Tulkarm
                Askar
No.1
Jalazone   Balata   Zarka
Amari   Karame
Deir Ammar   Jabal Hussein
Kalandya   Nuweimeh
         Aida Ein es Sult
Dheished   Mulaskar
Gaza Beach Beit   Agabat Jabr
Nusseirat   Djibrin Arrdub
Deir el Balah
Rafah   Jibalya   **JORDAN**
         El Bureij
         El Muazi   Fawwar
Khan Yunis

ISRAEL
R. Jordan

EGYPT   *Negev*

Sinai

© Martin Gilbert

56

THE ARABS OF NORTHERN ISRAEL

LEBANON

⊙ Arab and Druze villages in Israel

✪ Towns with mixed Arab and Jewish population

▮ Entirely Arab villages with more than 5,000 inhabitants

1949 CEASE-FIRE LINE

Jurdeih

Rihaniya

Jish

Tuba

Rama

SYRIA

Acre

Sakhnin

Maghar

Tamra

Arraba

Shefar Am

Haifa

Sea of Galilee

Kafr Kanna

Daliyat el Carmel

Nazareth

Fureidis

Umm el Fahm

Sandala

JORDAN

1949 CEASE-FIRE LINE

River Jordan

Baka

Mediterranean Sea

In 1949 some 160,000 Arabs remained in Israel. By 1966 their numbers had increased to 312,000, or 11% of the total population. Less than 6,000 Arabs left Israel during this period. From 1959, Arabs could join the Israeli Trade Union Organization, and on 1 December 1966 Israeli Military Government was abolished in all Arab areas. Since 1949, Arabs voted in all Israeli elections, and sent their own members to the Israeli Parliament. Since May 1948, both Hebrew and Arabic have been the official languages of the State of Israel, and three Arabic-language daily newspapers have been in regular production. But throughout this period, the Arabs maintained separate communities and cultural life, as did the 30,000 Bedouin who lived in the Negev and around Beersheba

al-Taiyiba

Tira

Jaljulya

Jaffa

The majority of the Arabs who remained in Israel after May 1948 lived in the northernmost part of the State. Whereas the Arabs who fled from Israel in 1948 were for the most part confined to refugee camps by their fellow Arab hosts and deliberately cut off from the economic development of the States in which they lived, the Arabs of Israel continued to live unmolested in their original homes, gained materially from Israel's own material successes, and received direct Israeli aid for irrigation, reclamation, mechanization and social welfare (including education, health and housing)

Lod

Karyat Jawarish   Ramla

0   5
Miles

© Martin Gilbert

NORTHERN ISRAEL AND THE GOLAN HEIGHTS 1949-1967

0 1 2 3 4 5
Miles

Mount Hermon

to Damascus

1000 metres

Metulla

Misgav Am

Margaliot

Majdal Shams

Banias

Kfar Giladi

Dan

Dafna

Masaada

LEBANON

Kiryat Shmona

Kfar Szold

Kfar Blum

Shamir

Yiftah

Lehavot Habashan

Kuneitra

Gonen

Ramot Naftali

Darbarshiye

Dishon

Yesod Hamaala

Kafar Naffakh

Hulata

Golan

Sde Eliezer

Gadot

Heights

Khushniye

Dalton

Hatzor Haglilit

Abu Fule

Rosh Pina

SYRIA

Safed

Kfar Hanasi

500 metres

Elifelet

Amiad

Almagor

Mahjar

Sheikh Ali

Khisfin

Migdal

Ginossar

Sea of

Tiberias

Galilee

200 metres

Ein Gev

Fik

Sharona

Poriya

Haon

Yarmuk

Kinneret

Yavniel

Degania

JORDAN

Shaar Hagolan

Massada

Tel Katzir

At the cease fire of 1949, Syria retained control of the Golan heights, which had been part of Syria since 1923. But instead of transforming this bleak region by cultivation, the Syrian Government fortified it, and used it as a base for repeated bombardments of Israeli settlements. Sixteen of these settlements were within two miles of the border. Despite the constant danger from bullets, mines and shells, the farmers continued to work their fields, while women and children accepted the dangers as a part of daily life

—·— The borders of Israel from 1949 to 1967

⁄⁄⁄ The Golan Heights: contour lines

⫽⫽⫽ Area within two miles of the Syrian border

⊙ Israeli settlements within two miles of the Syrian border

Syrian artillery range (ten miles)

• Israeli towns and settlements within Syrian artillery range of only 10 miles (Not all settlements are shown)

© Martin Gilbert

58

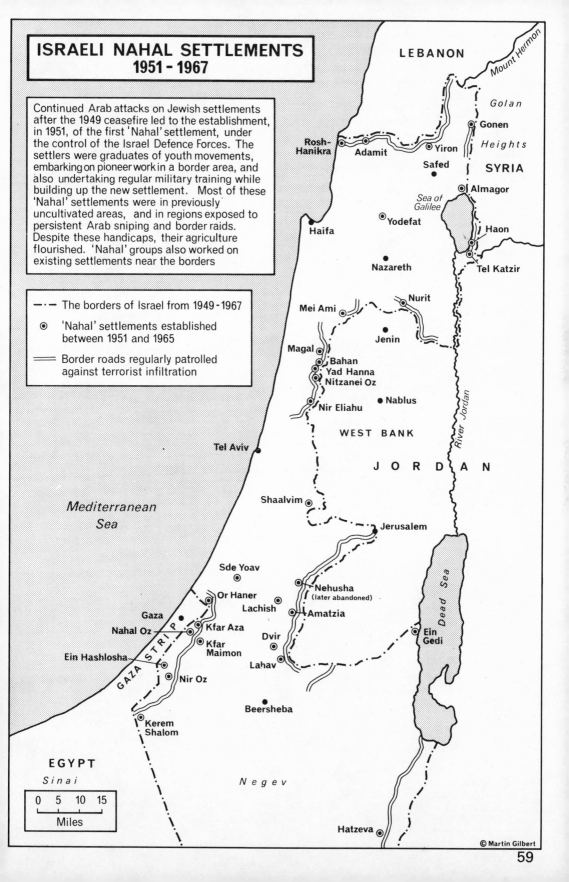

ISRAELI NAHAL SETTLEMENTS
1951 - 1967

Continued Arab attacks on Jewish settlements
after the 1949 ceasefire led to the establishment,
in 1951, of the first 'Nahal' settlement, under
the control of the Israel Defence Forces. The
settlers were graduates of youth movements,
embarking on pioneer work in a border area, and
also undertaking regular military training while
building up the new settlement. Most of these
'Nahal' settlements were in previously
uncultivated areas, and in regions exposed to
persistent Arab sniping and border raids.
Despite these handicaps, their agriculture
flourished. 'Nahal' groups also worked on
existing settlements near the borders

–·– The borders of Israel from 1949-1967

⊙ 'Nahal' settlements established
between 1951 and 1965

═══ Border roads regularly patrolled
against terrorist infiltration

LEBANON

Mount Hermon

Golan

Gonen

Rosh-
Hanikra   Adamit   Yiron   *Heights*

Safed   SYRIA

*Sea of
Galilee*   Almagor

Yodefat   Haon

Haifa   Tel Katzir

Nazareth

Nurit

Mei Ami   Jenin

Magal

Bahan
Yad Hanna
Nitzanei Oz

Nir Eliahu   Nablus

WEST BANK

River Jordan

Tel Aviv   J O R D A N

Shaalvim

*Mediterranean
Sea*

Jerusalem   *Dead
Sea*

Sde Yoav

Or Haner   Nehusha
Lachish   (later abandoned)

Gaza   Amatzia

Nahal Oz   Kfar Aza

Ein Hashlosha   Kfar   Dvir   Ein
Maimon   Gedi

Nir Oz   Lahav

Kerem
Shalom   Beersheba

EGYPT

Sinai   *Negev*

0   5   10   15
Miles

Hatzeva

© Martin Gilbert

TERRORIST RAIDS INTO ISRAEL
1951 - 1956

Palestinian terrorist groups, or Fedayeen, began systematic raids into Israel from 1950. Towards the end of 1954, the Egyptian Government supervised the formal establishment of Palestinian terrorist groups in the Gaza strip and north-eastern Sinai. Throughout 1955 an increasing number of raids were launched into Israel. From 1951 to 1956, Israeli vehicles were ambushed, farms attacked, fields boobytrapped and roads mined. Fedayeen from Gaza also infiltrated into Jordan, and operated from there. Saudi Arabia, Syria and Lebanon each gave the Fedayeen support and refuge. Local Jordanian-Palestinian Fedayeen were also active operating from the West Bank

ISRAELI DEATHS AS A RESULT OF FEDAYEEN ATTACKS		
YEAR	FROM	ISRAELI DEAD
1951	JORDAN	111
	EGYPT	26
1952	JORDAN	114
	EGYPT	48
1953	JORDAN	124
	EGYPT	38
1954	JORDAN	117
	EGYPT	50
1955	JORDAN	37
	EGYPT	241
1951-55	SYRIA	55
	LEBANON	6

◉   Centres of anti-Israel activity

↗   Moral and material support for Fedayeen attacks

➤   Movement of Fedayeen groups

▨   Areas of Fedayeen activity against Israel. With Egyptian encouragement, the Fedayeen also incited demonstrations inside Jordan against the Jordanian regime

Between 1951 and 1955 967 Israelis were killed by Arab terrorists operating inside Israel's 1949 borders

© Martin Gilbert

0 10 20 30 40 50
Miles

THE ISRAELI RESPONSE TO TERROR
1951 - 1966

In an attempt to halt terrorist activity, the Israeli Government organized a series of raids, first against villages sheltering terrorists (up to 1953), then against regular terrorist and Egyptian military units

LEBANON

Houle
29 APRIL 1966

Meiss el Jebel

The Golan Heights

SYRIA

Acre

Safed

2 MAY 1951

Haifa

Nuqeib

Tiberias

Tawafiq

1 FEB 1960

Shuna
27 MAY 1965

Jenin
27 MAY 1965

Mediterranean Sea

Netanya

Kalkiliya

10 - 11 OCT 1956
4 DEC 1965

Azzun

Tel Aviv

J O R D A N

Kibya   14 OCT 1953

Nilin   27 MARCH 1954

Beit Likya   2 SEPT 1954

Ashdod

Jerusalem

Husan
25 - 26 SEPT 1956

Gaza
28 FEB - 1 MAR 1955

Ar Rahwa

Samua

Dead Sea

Khan Yunis
31 AUG 1955

13 NOV
1966

Beersheba

11 SEPT 1956

Dimona

2 NOV 1955

Sabkha

E G Y P T

N e g e v

S i n a i

13 - 14 SEPT 1956

28 OCT 1955

Gharandal

Kuntilla

Eilat

– · – The borders of the State of Israel, 1949 - 1967

↑↗ Principal direction of terrorist infiltration

▨ Main areas of terrorist activity

⇗ Main counter-terrorist attacks, with dates

| 0 | 10 | 20 | 30 |
Miles

© Martin Gilbert

61

THE CHANGING BALANCE OF POWER IN THE ARAB WORLD
1953 – 1973

During the 1950's Britain and France were to a large extent eased out of the Arab world, and were partially replaced by the United States. But by the 1970's it was the Soviet Union which had gained the greatest influence

Nouasseur
United States
EVACUATED 1963

Kenitra
United States
LARGELY EVACUATED 1963

MOROCCO

Mers-el-Kebir
France
EVACUATED 1963

Bizerta
France
EVACUATED 1963

TUNISIA

Mediterranean Sea

El-Adhem
British
EVACUATED 1970

Wheelus
United States
EVACUATED 1970

Tobruk
British
EVACUATED 197

A L G E R I A

L I B Y A

British and French influence in the Arab world was greatly weakened in 1956, after British troops landed at Port Said, in an unsuccessful attempt to reverse, by force, Egypt's nationalisation of the Suez Canal

| 0 | 100 | 200 | 300 | 400 |
Miles

- ● Western naval and air bases (French, British and United States) in existence in 1953, but abandoned by 1973

- ◉ Soviet naval bases and facilities established between 1963 and 1973

- ☀ British air base (in Cyprus) whose use was denied to the United States by Britain during the Middle East war of October 1973

- Arab countries which received the majority of their arms from the Soviet Union, 1971 - 1973

- Other Arab countries receiving Soviet military aid since 1967

VALUE OF SOVIET ARMS SUPPLIE 1965 - 1970 (in dollars)	
Egypt	$4,500 millio
Iraq	$500 millio
Syria	$450 millio
Algeria	$250 millio
Others (Sudan, South Yemen, Yemen, Libya)	$1,000 millio
Total	$6,700 millio

© Martin Gilbert

62

THE SOVIET UNION

DATE OF FIRST SOVIET
ARMS AGREEMENT WITH:

EGYPT	1955
SYRIA	1955
IRAQ	1958
YEMEN	1958
ALGERIA	1962
SUDAN	1967
SOUTH YEMEN	1967
LIBYA	1970

Black Sea

Caspian Sea

TURKEY

Latakia
SYRIA
Akrotiri

Habbaniya
British
EVACUATED 1959

I R A Q

Shuayba
British
EVACUATED
1959

From 1968 to Sept 1973 the Soviet
Union sent the Arab States
2,603 million dollars worth of
arms. During that same period
the United States sent the Arab
States 803 million dollars worth
of arms, and a further 867 million
dollars worth of direct economic
aid. From 1968 to 1973 the United
States also sent Israel 1,352 million
dollars worth of arms and 420
million dollars of economic aid

ISRAEL
1967 borders

KUWAIT

Mersa

Alexandria
Port Said

Canal Zone
British
EVACUATED 1954

E G Y P T

Bahrein
British
EVACUATED 1971
United States naval
facilities CANCELLED 1974

Persian Gulf

MUSCAT

AND

OMAN

Masira

Ras Banas

S A U D I
A R A B I A

Red

Port Sudan

Sea

S U D A N

SOUTH
YEMEN

*Arabian
Sea*

YEMEN
Hudeida

Aden

Socotra

Berbera

SOMALIA

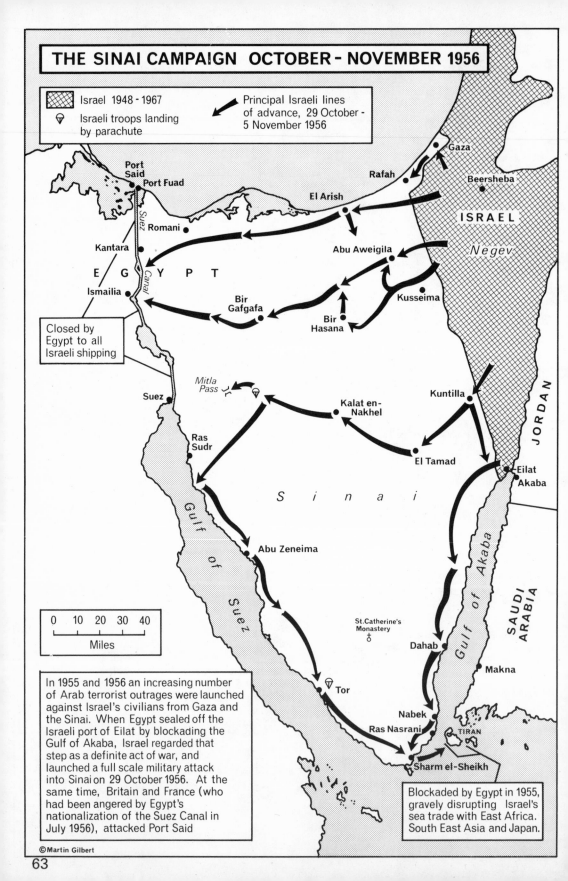

THE SINAI CAMPAIGN OCTOBER – NOVEMBER 1956

Legend:
- Israel 1948 - 1967
- Israeli troops landing by parachute
- Principal Israeli lines of advance, 29 October – 5 November 1956

**Labels on map:**

Gaza

Beersheba

Port Said

Port Fuad

Rafah

El Arish

ISRAEL

Romani

Kantara

Abu Aweigila

Negev

E G Y P T

Ismailia

Bir Gafgafa

Kusseima

Bir Hasana

Closed by Egypt to all Israeli shipping

Suez Canal

Mitla Pass

Kalat en-Nakhel

Kuntilla

JORDAN

Suez

Ras Sudr

El Tamad

Eilat
Akaba

S i n a i

Gulf of Suez

Abu Zeneima

St.Catherine's Monastery

Gulf of Akaba

Dahab

Makna

SAUDI ARABIA

Scale:

0 10 20 30 40

Miles

Tor

Nabek

Ras Nasrani

TIRAN

Sharm el-Sheikh

In 1955 and 1956 an increasing number of Arab terrorist outrages were launched against Israel's civilians from Gaza and the Sinai. When Egypt sealed off the Israeli port of Eilat by blockading the Gulf of Akaba, Israel regarded that step as a definite act of war, and launched a full scale military attack into Sinai on 29 October 1956. At the same time, Britain and France (who had been angered by Egypt's nationalization of the Suez Canal in July 1956), attacked Port Said

Blockaded by Egypt in 1955, gravely disrupting Israel's sea trade with East Africa, South East Asia and Japan.

© Martin Gilbert

THE ISRAELI WITHDRAWAL FROM SINAI MARCH 1957

As a result of pressure from both the United Nations and the United States, Israeli forces withdrew from Sinai in March 1957. A United Nations force of 3,300 men took up positions in Gaza, at Sharm el-Sheikh and along the Sinai border, in order to secure that border against attack, and to prevent Egypt re-blockading the Gulf of Akaba. But despite Israel's withdrawal, the Egyptians refused to open the Suez Canal to Israeli shipping, and continued to allow Gaza to be used as a base for terrorist raids inside Israel

Before Israel withdrew from the Gaza Strip she was assured that Egyptian troops would not return. But Egypt moved her forces into Gaza within 48 hours of the Israeli withdrawal. At the same time as the Israeli withdrawal, British troops left Port Said and French forces withdrew from Port Fuad

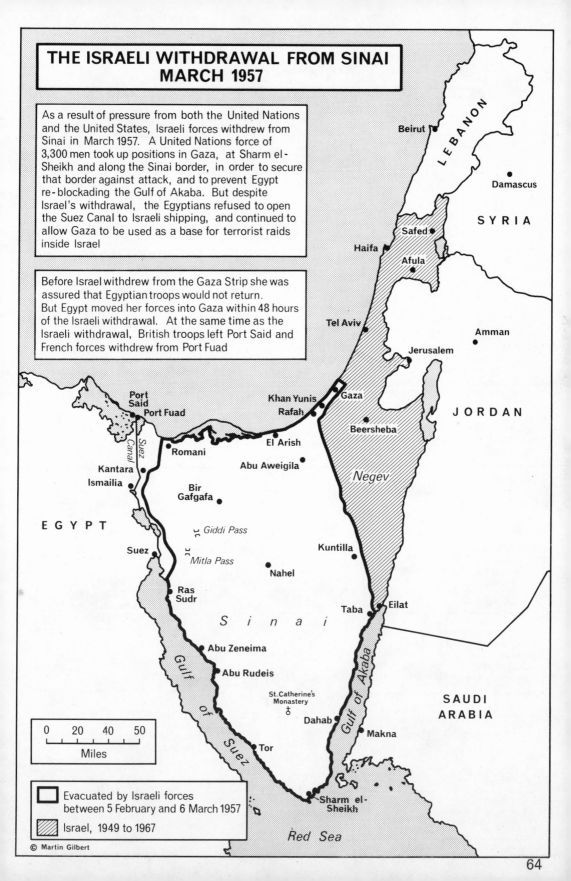

LEBANON

Beirut

Damascus

SYRIA

Safed

Haifa

Afula

Tel Aviv

Amman

Jerusalem

JORDAN

Port Said
Port Fuad

Khan Yunis
Rafah

Gaza

Beersheba

Suez Canal

El Arish

Romani

Negev

Kantara

Abu Aweigila

Ismailia

Bir Gafgafa

EGYPT

Giddi Pass

Mitla Pass

Kuntilla

Suez

Nahel

Ras Sudr

Taba

Eilat

S i n a i

Abu Zeneima

Gulf of Suez

Abu Rudeis

Gulf of Akaba

St. Catherine's Monastery

SAUDI ARABIA

Dahab

Makna

0	20	40	50

Miles

Tor

Evacuated by Israeli forces between 5 February and 6 March 1957

Israel, 1949 to 1967

Sharm el-Sheikh

Red Sea

© Martin Gilbert

SYRIAN ACTIVITY AGAINST ISRAELI SETTLEMENTS FEBRUARY - OCTOBER 1966

0 1 2 3 4 5
Miles

6 September 7 land reclamation officers wounded by a mine

Shear Yashuv

S Y R I A

L E B A N O N

30 April 4 Israeli workers wounded by Syrian machine gun fire
5 June Syrians shell workers in the fields
6 June Syrian shells set fire to fields

Ashmura
Hulata

13 February Syrians shoot at Israeli tractors with mortars. Israeli forces succeed in putting two Syrian tanks out of action

The border between Syria and Israel was the scene of repeated Syrian bombardment, sniping and minelaying between 1948 and 1967. From their fortifications on the Golan heights, the Syrians tried to disrupt the daily life of the Israeli farmers and fishermen.

Gadot

Mahanayim

12 July A tractor driver seriously wounded by a Syrian mine

River Jordan

12 July An afforestation officer killed by a Syrian mine

Almagor

In 1963, at the instigation of the Arab League, Syria tried to divert the head-waters of the Jordan, so that Israel would lose her main source of freshwater, and be unable to complete her plans to harness the Jordan waters for irrigation works throughout Israel. In 1964 Israeli artillery destroyed the Syrian earth-digging equipment which was about to begin the diversion, and Syrian plans were abandoned

26 September Syrians fire on a fishing boat

21 February Syrians fire mortar shells at a patrol escorting fisherman on lake
15 August Syrians open fire on patrol boat. Israelis retaliate. 5 Israeli soldiers wounded. Two Syrian planes shot down

Sea
of
Galilee

We shall never call for nor accept peace. We shall only accept war. We have resolved to drench this land with your blood, to oust you aggressors, to throw you into the sea HAFIZ ASSAD, THEN SYRIAN DEFENCE MINISTER, 24 MAY 1966

Haon

22 February Syrians fire on a tractor
29 March Tractor driver wounded by Syrian machine gun fire
30 March A second tractor driver wounded by Syrian artillery fire
22 October Tractor driver fired at

Shaar Hagolan

I S R A E L

Jordan

Our Army will be satisfied with nothing less than the disappearance of Israel, SALAH JADID, SYRIAN CHIEF OF STAFF 30 OCTOBER 1964

J O R D A N

9 October 4 border policemen killed by a Syrian mine

River

© Martin Gilbert

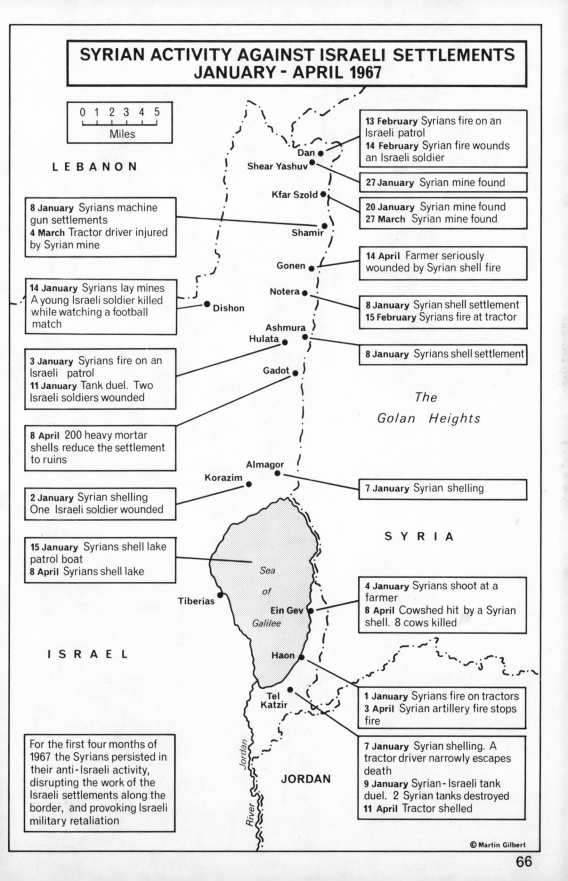

SYRIAN ACTIVITY AGAINST ISRAELI SETTLEMENTS
JANUARY - APRIL 1967

0 1 2 3 4 5
Miles

LEBANON

13 February Syrians fire on an Israeli patrol
14 February Syrian fire wounds an Israeli soldier

27 January Syrian mine found

20 January Syrian mine found
27 March Syrian mine found

Dan
Shear Yashuv

Kfar Szold

8 January Syrians machine gun settlements
4 March Tractor driver injured by Syrian mine

Shamir

14 April Farmer seriously wounded by Syrian shell fire

Gonen

Notera

8 January Syrian shell settlement
15 February Syrians fire at tractor

14 January Syrians lay mines A young Israeli soldier killed while watching a football match

● Dishon

Ashmura
Hulata

8 January Syrians shell settlement

3 January Syrians fire on an Israeli patrol
11 January Tank duel. Two Israeli soldiers wounded

Gadot

The Golan Heights

8 April 200 heavy mortar shells reduce the settlement to ruins

Almagor

Korazim

7 January Syrian shelling

2 January Syrian shelling One Israeli soldier wounded

SYRIA

15 January Syrians shell lake patrol boat
8 April Syrians shell lake

Sea of Galilee

4 January Syrians shoot at a farmer
8 April Cowshed hit by a Syrian shell. 8 cows killed

Tiberias

Ein Gev

ISRAEL

Haon

1 January Syrians fire on tractors
3 April Syrian artillery fire stops fire

Tel Katzir

For the first four months of 1967 the Syrians persisted in their anti-Israeli activity, disrupting the work of the Israeli settlements along the border, and provoking Israeli military retaliation

JORDAN

River Jordan

7 January Syrian shelling. A tractor driver narrowly escapes death
9 January Syrian-Israeli tank duel. 2 Syrian tanks destroyed
11 April Tractor shelled

© Martin Gilbert

66

THE MIDDLE EAST CRISIS
14-24 MAY 1967

0 20 40 60 80
Miles

■ The State of Israel, 1949-1967

◉ United Nations troops acting as a buffer force in the Sinai Peninsula and the Gaza Strip

LEBANON
12,000 Troops
80 Tanks
18 Combat Aircraft

IRAQ
70,000 Troops
400 Tanks
200 Combat Aircraft

SYRIA
50,000 Troops
400 Tanks
120 Combat Aircraft

TOTAL ARAB STRENGTH
547,000 Troops
2,504 Tanks
957 Combat Aircraft

ISRAEL
264,000 Troops
800 Tanks
300 Combat Aircraft

Beirut

Damascus

Kuneitra

Jerusalem

Amman

KUWAIT
5,000 Troops
24 Tanks
9 Combat Aircraft

Port Said

Gaza

El Arish

Abu Aweigila

Cairo

Suez

Suez Canal

Kuntilla

JORDAN
50,000 Troops
200 Tanks
40 Combat Aircraft

Eilat   Akaba

Sinai

SAUDI ARABIA
50,000 Troops
100 Tanks
20 Combat Aircraft

EGYPT
240,000 Troops
1,200 Tanks
500 Combat Aircraft

Dahab

Makna

Strait of Tiran

CHRONOLOGY OF THE CRISIS

14 May: Egypt mobilizes

16 May: Egyptian forces move eastwards across Sinai

16 May: Egypt demands withdrawal of all United Nations forces

19 May: United Nations forces withdraw. Cairo radio announces: *'This is our chance Arabs, to deal Israel a mortal blow of annihilation, to blot out its entire presence in our holy land'*

22 May: Cairo radio announces: *'The Arab people is firmly resolved to wipe Israel off the map'.* Egypt declares the Strait of Tiran closed to all Israeli shipping

UNITED NATIONS FORCE
978 Indians
795 Canadians
579 Yugoslavs
530 Swedes
430 Brazilians
61 Norwegians

Sharm el Sheikh

Red Sea

ALGERIA
60,000 Troops
400 Tanks
100 Combat Aircraft

© Martin Gilbert

THE MIDDLE EAST CRISIS 25 – 30 MAY 1967

Our basic objective will be the destruction of Israel. The Arab people want to fight.... The mining of Sharm el Sheikh is a confrontation with Israel. Adopting this measure obligates us to be ready to embark on a general war with Israel **PRESIDENT NASSER OF EGYPT, 27 MAY 1967**

On 25 May 1967, encouraged to do so by Egypt, the Governments of Syria, Iraq, Jordan and Saudi Arabia moved their troops to Israel's borders. This was the first time since the armistice agreements of 1949 that Arab armies had gathered in such large numbers. The movement of troops was accompanied by an outburst of anti-Israeli statements by the Arab leaders and by their Government-controlled radios, which convinced the Israelis that war was imminent

Mediterranean Sea

Beirut

LEBANON

S Y R I A

Damascus

Haifa

I R A Q

Tel Aviv

Jerusalem

Amman

Gaza

ISRAEL

Port Said

El Arish

Suez Canal

E G Y P T

Negev

JORDAN

SAUDI ARABIA

Abu Aweigila

Kuntilla

Suez

Eilat

Akaba

S i n a i

Dahab

With the closing of the Gulf of Akaba, Israel is faced with two alternatives either of which will destroy it; it will either be strangled to death by the Arab military and economic boycott, or it will perish by the fire of the Arab forces encompassing it from the South from the North and from the East **CAIRO RADIO 30 MAY 1967**

Makna

The State of Israel, 1949 - 1967

Sharm el Sheikh

Straits of Tiran

Hurghada

Israeli ships not able to proceed because of Egyptian naval blockade (the Suez Canal had been closed to Israeli ships since the foundation of Israel in 1948)

Red Sea

Wajh

Quseir

Movement of Arab armies to Israel's borders, including movements across Sinai (from which the United Nations' buffer force had withdrawn on Egyptian insistence)

0	20	40	60	80

Miles

© Martin Gilbert

68

THE MIDDLE EAST CRISIS 31 MAY – 5 JUNE 1967

By 31 May 1967 Egypt had moved 100,000 troops, 1000 tanks and 500 heavy guns into the Sinai 'buffer zone'.   By 4 June Israel was outnumbered three-to-one by the Arab forces on borders. Egyptian ships continued to blockade the Strait of Tiran, and Egypt refused to lift the blockade. On 5 June Israel decided to pre-empt an Arab attack, and struck at air bases throughout Egypt

■ The State of Israel, 1949–1967

◉ Egyptian air bases attacked by Israeli planes on the morning of 5 June 1967

Mediterranean   Sea

LEBANON

Beirut

Damascus

SYRIA

Haifa

Tel Aviv
Kalkilya
Jerusalem
Amman

Gaza

ISRAEL

JORDAN

Port Said

El Mansura
Inchas
Deir Suweir
El Arish
Gebel Libni

Abu Suweir
Bir Gafgafa

Cairo International
Fayid
Kabrit
Bir Thamada

Cairo West
Almaza
Suez
Helwan

Eilat
Akaba

Sinai

Beni Suef

E G Y P T

El Minya

Dahab

SAUDI ARABIA

Makna

Sharm el Sheikh

Straits of Tiran

Hurghada

Nile

Red   Sea

Under terms of the military agreement signed with Jordan, Jordanian artillery co-ordinated with the forces of Egypt and Syria is in a position to cut Israel in two at Kalkilya, where Israeli territory between the Jordan armistice line and the Mediterranean Sea is only twelve kilometres wide.... **EL AKHBAR NEWSPAPER, CAIRO, 31 MAY 1967**

The existence of Israel is an error which must be rectified. This is our opportunity to wipe out the ignominy which has been with us since 1948. Our goal is clear – to wipe Israel off the map **PRESIDENT AREF OF IRAQ, 31 MAY 1967**

This is a fight for the homeland – it is either us or the Israelis. There is no middle road. The Jews of Palestine will have to leave. We will facilitate their departure to their former homes Any of the old Palestine Jewish population who survive may stay, but it is my impression that none of them will survive **AHMED SHUKAIRY, CHAIRMAN OF THE PALESTINE LIBERATION ORGANIZATION 1 JUNE 1967**

Luxor

0 20 40 60 80
Miles

Ras Banas

© Martin Gilbert

69

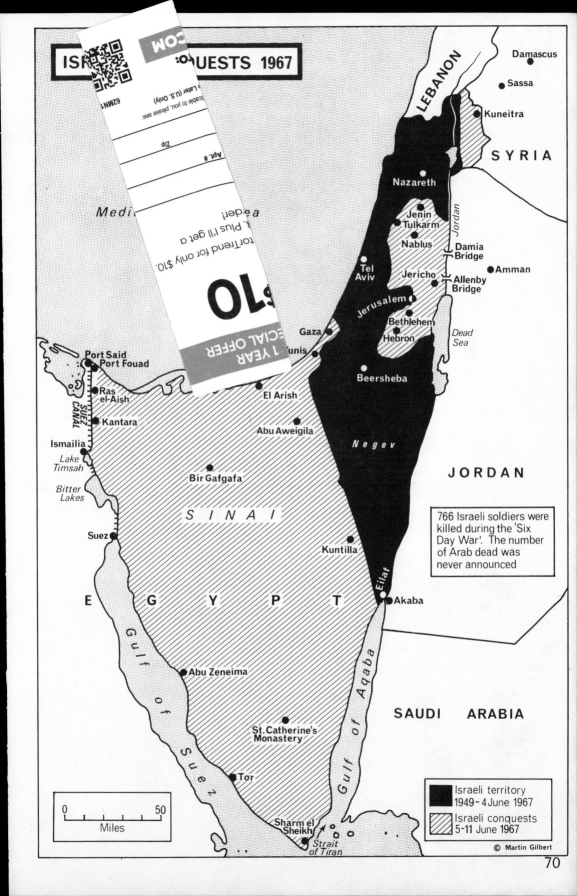

ISRAELI CONQUESTS 1967

LEBANON

Damascus
Sassa
Kuneitra

SYRIA

Nazareth

Jenin
Tulkarm
Nablus

Damia Bridge

Amman

Tel Aviv

Jericho
Jerusalem
Allenby Bridge

Bethlehem
Hebron

Dead Sea

Gaza

Negev

Beersheba

JORDAN

Mediterranean

Port Said
Port Fouad
Ras el-Aish

El Arish

Abu Aweigila

Kantara

Ismailia

Lake Timsah

Bir Gafgafa

Bitter Lakes

S I N A I

Suez

Kuntilla

766 Israeli soldiers were killed during the 'Six Day War'. The number of Arab dead was never announced

E G Y P T

Eilat
Akaba

Abu Zeneima

SAUDI ARABIA

St. Catherine's Monastery

Tor

Sharm el Sheikh

Gulf of Suez

Gulf of Aqaba

Strait of Tiran

■ Israeli territory 1949–4 June 1967

▨ Israeli conquests 5-11 June 1967

© Martin Gilbert

0 ____ 50
Miles

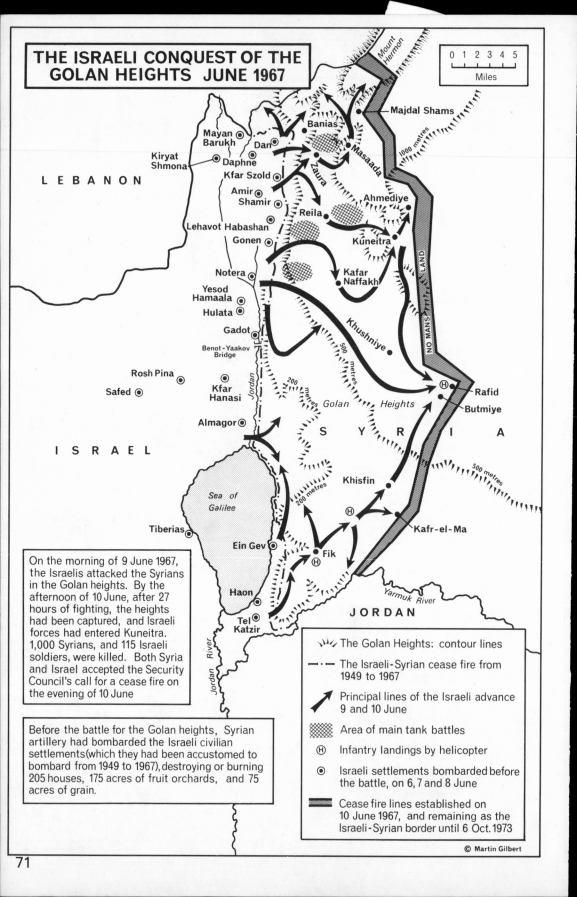

THE ISRAELI CONQUEST OF THE GOLAN HEIGHTS JUNE 1967

LEBANON

ISRAEL

SYRIA

JORDAN

Mount Hermon

Majdal Shams

Banias
Masaada

Mayan Barukh
Dan
Kiryat Shmona
Daphne
Kfar Szold
Amir
Shamir
Zaura
Reila
Ahmediye
Lehavot Habashan
Gonen
Kuneitra
Notera
Kafar Naffakh
Yesod Hamaala
Hulata
Gadot
Benot-Yaakov Bridge
Khushniye
Rosh Pina
Kfar Hanasi
Safed
Almagor

Jordan

1000 metres
NO MANS LAND
500 metres
200 metres
Golan Heights
500 metres
200 metres

Rafid
Butmiye

Sea of Galilee

Tiberias
Ein Gev
Haon
Tel Katzir

Khisfin
Fik
Kafr-el-Ma

Yarmuk River

Jordan River

0 1 2 3 4 5
Miles

On the morning of 9 June 1967, the Israelis attacked the Syrians in the Golan heights. By the afternoon of 10 June, after 27 hours of fighting, the heights had been captured, and Israeli forces had entered Kuneitra. 1,000 Syrians, and 115 Israeli soldiers, were killed. Both Syria and Israel accepted the Security Council's call for a cease fire on the evening of 10 June

Before the battle for the Golan heights, Syrian artillery had bombarded the Israeli civilian settlements (which they had been accustomed to bombard from 1949 to 1967), destroying or burning 205 houses, 175 acres of fruit orchards, and 75 acres of grain.

⌇⌇⌇ The Golan Heights: contour lines

—·— The Israeli-Syrian cease fire from 1949 to 1967

↗ Principal lines of the Israeli advance 9 and 10 June

▦ Area of main tank battles

Ⓗ Infantry landings by helicopter

◉ Israeli settlements bombarded before the battle, on 6, 7 and 8 June

▰▰ Cease fire lines established on 10 June 1967, and remaining as the Israeli-Syrian border until 6 Oct. 1973

© Martin Gilbert

71

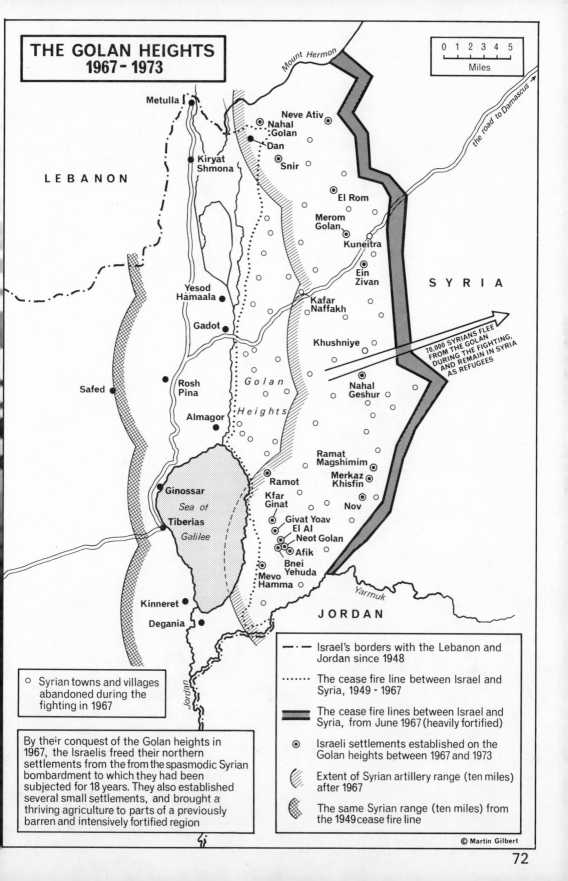

THE GOLAN HEIGHTS
1967 - 1973

Mount Hermon

the road to Damascus →

0 1 2 3 4 5
Miles

Metulla

Neve Ativ

Nahal
Golan

Dan

Kiryat
Shmona

Snir

L E B A N O N

El Rom

Merom
Golan

Kuneitra

Ein
Zivan

S Y R I A

Yesod
Hamaala

Kafar
Naffakh

Gadot

Khushniye

70,000 SYRIANS FLEE
FROM THE GOLAN
DURING THE FIGHTING,
AND REMAIN IN SYRIA
AS REFUGEES

Safed

Rosh
Pina

Golan

Nahal
Geshur

Almagor

Heights

Ramat
Magshimim

Ramot

Merkaz
Khisfin

Kfar
Ginat

Nov

Ginossar

Sea of

Givat Yoav

El Al

Tiberias

Neot Golan

Galilee

Afik

Bnei
Yehuda

Mevo
Hamma

Yarmuk

Kinneret

J O R D A N

Degania

Jordan

○ Syrian towns and villages
abandoned during the
fighting in 1967

By their conquest of the Golan heights in
1967, the Israelis freed their northern
settlements from the from the spasmodic Syrian
bombardment to which they had been
subjected for 18 years. They also established
several small settlements, and brought a
thriving agriculture to parts of a previously
barren and intensively fortified region

—·— Israel's borders with the Lebanon and
Jordan since 1948

········ The cease fire line between Israel and
Syria, 1949 - 1967

▨ The cease fire lines between Israel and
Syria, from June 1967 (heavily fortified)

⊙ Israeli settlements established on the
Golan heights between 1967 and 1973

◖ Extent of Syrian artillery range (ten miles)
after 1967

◖ The same Syrian range (ten miles) from
the 1949 cease fire line

© Martin Gilbert

72

THE GAZA STRIP: A BASE FOR TERROR
1967 – 1972

0   1   2
Miles

From 1949 to 1967 the Egyptians confined the refugees of the 1948 war to refugee camps, and distributed violently anti-Israeli and anti-semitic propaganda. After 1967 Israel allowed free movement out of camps, both for visits to Jordan and other Arab countries, and for work in Israel. From 1968 to 1971 the Gaza Strip was the main base for Arab terrorists, who attacked nearby Israeli settlements, and who also killed Arabs in the Strip who had cooperated or worked with the Israelis. By mid-1972 the terrorist networks had been broken, and terrorism was limited to spasmodic incidents

Karmiya
Zikkim
Yad Mordechai
Erez
Beit Lahiya
Jibalya
Nazla
Beit Hanun
Gaza
Nir Am
Mefalsim
Nahal Netzarim
Kfar Aza
Saad
Nahal Oz
Alumim
El Bureij
Kfar Maimon
Nusseirat
Beeri
Shokeda
El Muazi
Deir el Balah
Nahal Kfar Darom
Reim
Mediterranean Sea
Kisufim
Ein Hashlosha
Nirim
Khan Yunis
Abasan
Nir Oz
Magen
Nahal Morag
Amioz
Yesha
Rafah
Nir Yitzhak
Mivtahim
Sadot
Kerem Shalom
Minyan
SINAI
OCCUPIED BY ISRAEL
IN 1967

ARAB CIVILIANS KILLED BY ARAB TERRORISTS IN THE GAZA STRIP	
Men	84
Women	33
Children under 14	21
Total killed	138
Total wounded	1,199

— · — Border of the Gaza Strip, occupied by Egypt (1948 to 1967) and by Israel (1967 –

◼ Principal towns of the Gaza Strip

▨ Main centres of terrorist recruitment and training

⊙ Israeli settlements frequently attacked by terrorists from Gaza

ʌʌʌ Security fences, by which the Israel Defence Forces sought to seal off the Gaza Strip from terrorist movement into Israeli settlements

⊕ Israeli settlements established between 1967 and 1973

➤ Israeli military action in mid-1972 to break the terrorist networks

© Martin Gilbert

TERRORIST ACTIVITY AGAINST ISRAEL JUNE 1967 – DECEMBER 1968

0   10   20
Miles

Between June 1967 and December 1968 there were 159 terrorist raids deep inside Israel, mostly directed against busy civilian centres such as bus stations and markets. During this period 47 Israeli civilians were killed and 330 injured. A further 1029 raids took place in border areas. In these, and on the counter-terrorist operations, 234 Israeli soldiers were killed and 785 injured

AN ISRAELI CIVILIAN SETTLEMENT 1968: A TYPICAL BORDER STORY

22 Jan: Bazooka shelling, 2 wounded

11 Feb: Shelling

12 Feb: 2 soldiers wounded clearing mines

15 Feb: Shelling. Dining hall, milking shed and childrens' home damaged

13 June: Shelling. 6 farmers wounded Crops, fields set on fire

LEBANON

SYRIA

The Golan Heights

■ Zebdani

El Hamma ■   ■ Duma
■ Damascus

■ Nawa

■ Safed

Sea of Galilee

Haifa

Nazareth

Gesher

Irbid ■   ■ Deraa
■ Ramtha

Mediterranean Sea

Katabiya

Tayasir

Nablus

Beit Furik

Tel Aviv

Ramallah

Jerusalem

Bethlehem

Muaskar el Arub

Hebron

● Mafrak

Ajlun
Kureima   ■ Jerash

J O R D A N

Salt ■   ● Zarqa

Karame   ■ Amman

Jordan

Dead Sea

22 November 1968   A Palestinian terrorist bomb exploded in the Mahane Yehuda market in Jerusalem, killing 12 Jews and 2 Arabs. One of the Arabs was a boy of 11, the other an old man of 71

As a result of the Six Day War, Israel occupied the Jordanian territory west of the Jordan river. Before 1967 this area had been a centre for Palestinian terrorist raids into Israel. From June 1967 to December 1968 the terrorists sought to establish permanent bases inside the Israeli occupied West Bank, hoping to advance from sporadic terrorism to mass guerilla activity. Syria assisted their training. Iraq and Jordan facilitated their transport. Egypt and Algeria encouraged recruitment. By December 1968 the Israelis had defeated all but a small handfull of these West Bank terrorists, the majority of whom were captured and imprisoned

– · – Israel's borders, 1967 - 1973

▨ The West Bank, administered by Israel, June 1967-

■ Terrorist training and transit camps outside Israel

◤ Main terrorist routes

⊙ Centres used by terrorists inside the West Bank

© Martin Gilbert

ISRAELI SECURITY MEASURES AND THE JORDAN VALLEY
1967 – 1970

⊙ Israeli military settlements (Nahal settlements) established 1967 - 1969

ƺ Main Israeli border defences (forts, mine-fields, artillery units) established 1968-1970

⊐⊏ Bridges open to Arab civilian trade and traffic in both directions, and across which Arabs suspected of terrorism were expelled

◗ Main areas of terrorist activity, June - December 1967

Main terrorist bases, for frequent raids across the Jordan, January - March 1968

Main terrorist bases (after the Karame raid) used for spasmodic raids across the Jordan, April 1968 - September 1970

■ Towns and villages in which the Israeli military authorities blew up Arab houses between June 1967 and November 1969, as reprisals against terrorist activity. In ail, more than 5,000 houses were destroyed, and more than five hundred Arabs expelled from the West Bank. By October 1973 more than a thousand Arabs had been expelled

–·– The Israel - Jordan cease-fire line established in June 1967

······ The 'Green Line' cease-fire line between Israel and Jordan from 1949 to 1967

Armed struggle is the only way to liberate Palestine.... the liberation of Palestine is a national duty to repulse the Zionist, imperialist invasion from the great Arab homeland and to purge the Zionist presence from Palestine.... the partition of Palestine in 1947 and the establishment of Israel are fundamentally null and void.
THE PALESTINE NATIONAL COVENANT, adopted 17 JULY 1968 by the Palestine National Council

Afula

Irbid

Jenin

Tulkarm

Tubas

Ajlun

Nablus

Kalkiliya

Nahal Gitit ⊙
Nahal Massua ⊙

R. Jordan

WEST BANK

Nahal Hagilgal ⊙

Salt

Nahal Naaran ⊙

Tel Aviv

ISRAEL

Karame

Beit Nuba   Ramallah
         Yalu   Bira
Latrun

Nahal Kallia

Amman

JORDAN

Imwas

East Jerusalem

Mediterranean Sea

Ashdod

Jebel Khalil   Halhoul

Beit Auwa   Hebron

Mirsim

Dead Sea

0   5   10   15

Miles

Between 1967 and 1970, Arab terrorists on the West Bank killed 12 Israelis, as well as over 50 Arabs whom they accused of 'collaborating' with Israel. Israeli forces were active in driving the terrorists towards the Jordan river, and on 21 March 1968 crossed the river in force to attack the terrorist base at Karame. Following this raid, the Israeli army established a fortified line along the Jordan, with a border fence and minefields, effectively sealing the border, and the terrorists themselves withdrew eastwards from the valley to the mountains. During 1970 terrorist acts on the West Bank stopped almost completely. They began again, on a smale scale, after October 1973

THE WEST BANK UNDER ISRAELI MILITARY ADMINISTRATION 1967–

The Israeli conquest of the West Bank in June 1967 brought 600,000 Arabs under Israeli military administration. The Israelis encouraged and financed economic development, and by the end of 1970 Arab unemployment had dropped from 12% to 3%. By 1972 over 60,000 Arabs crossed the 'Green Line' every morning to work in Israel. At the same time, over 100,000 Arabs visited other Arab states for work, education and business. By 1973 over 14,500 West Bank Arabs were working in local administration in the West Bank

Sixteen Israeli settlements were founded in the West Bank between 1967 and 1973, with a total civilian population of 1,150. One of these settlements was near Hebron, where Jews had lived for more than two thousand years, before being driven out by the Arabs in 1929. Another group of settlements, the Etzion Bloc, was established on the site of settlements destroyed by the Arabs in 1949. At the same time, 44,000 Arabs who had fled from the West Bank in 1967, returned by 1972

During 1970 an 'Open Bridges' policy enabled West Bank Arabs to cross freely into Jordan. At the height of the tourist season in 1970, some 750 buses a day crossed from Jordan to Hebron, and by the end of August 50,000 Arabs had visited the West Bank from Jordan

ARABS VISITING THE WEST BANK FROM OTHER ARAB AREAS	
1968	16,000
1969	23,000
1970	52,000
1971	107,000
1972	150,000

Mediterranean Sea

Jenin

Mehola

Tulkarm

Tubas

Bekaot

Nablus

Hamra

Argaman

Kalkilya

Nahal Mehora

Nahal Gitit

Nahal Massua

Damiya Bridge

Maaleh Efraim

ISRAEL

JORDAN

Nahal Hagilgal

Um-e-Shurt Bridge

Nahal Naaran

Mundasa Bridge

Ramallah · Bira

Allenby Bridge

Jericho

River Jordan

Nahal Kallia

Abdullah Bridge

West Jerusalem

East Jerusalem

Merkaz Alon Shevut

Bethlehem

Rosh Tzurim

Kfar Etzion

Nahal Mizpeh Shalem

Dead Sea

Hebron

Kiryat Arba

0	5

Miles

– · – The border between Jordan and Israel, 1967

■■■ The 'Green Line', Israel's border with Jordan, 1949–1967

◉ Israeli settlements established in the 'administered territories' between 1967 and 1973

✪ Principal Arab towns on the West Bank

○ Main Arab villages

© Martin Gilbert

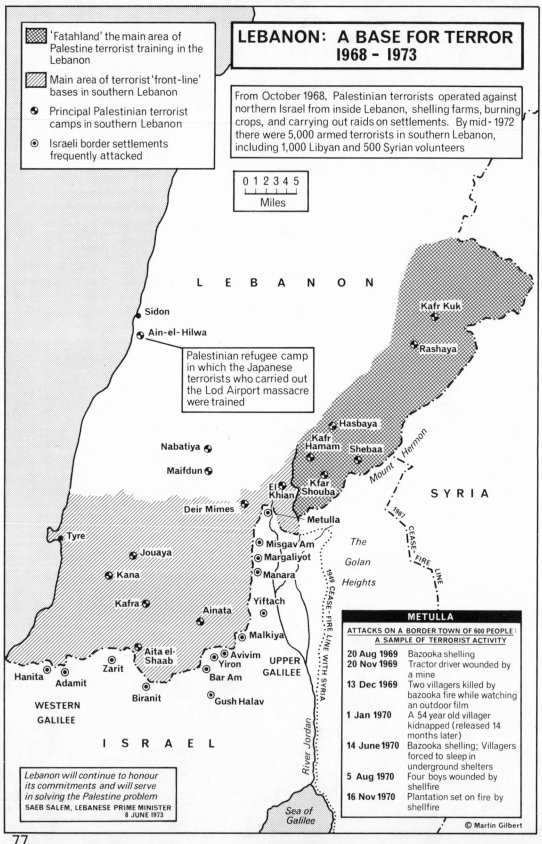

LEGEND

'Fatahland' the main area of Palestine terrorist training in the Lebanon

Main area of terrorist 'front-line' bases in southern Lebanon

Principal Palestinian terrorist camps in southern Lebanon

Israeli border settlements frequently attacked

LEBANON: A BASE FOR TERROR 1968 - 1973

From October 1968, Palestinian terrorists operated against northern Israel from inside Lebanon, shelling farms, burning crops, and carrying out raids on settlements. By mid-1972 there were 5,000 armed terrorists in southern Lebanon, including 1,000 Libyan and 500 Syrian volunteers

0 1 2 3 4 5
Miles

L E B A N O N

Sidon

Ain-el-Hilwa

Palestinian refugee camp in which the Japanese terrorists who carried out the Lod Airport massacre were trained

Kafr Kuk

Rashaya

Hasbaya

Kafr Hamam

Shebaa

Nabatiya

Maifdun

El Khian

Kfar Shouba

Mount Hermon

S Y R I A

Deir Mimes

Metulla

1967 CEASE FIRE LINE

Tyre

Misgav Am

Jouaya

Margaliyot

Kana

Manara

The Golan Heights

Kafra

Yiftach

Ainata

Malkiya

1949 CEASE-FIRE LINE WITH SYRIA

Aita el-Shaab

Avivim

Yiron

UPPER GALILEE

Hanita

Zarit

Bar Am

Adamit

Biranit

Gush Halav

WESTERN GALILEE

I S R A E L

River Jordan

METULLA	
ATTACKS ON A BORDER TOWN OF 600 PEOPLE: A SAMPLE OF TERRORIST ACTIVITY	
20 Aug 1969	Bazooka shelling
20 Nov 1969	Tractor driver wounded by a mine
13 Dec 1969	Two villagers killed by bazooka fire while watching an outdoor film
1 Jan 1970	A 54 year old villager kidnapped (released 14 months later)
14 June 1970	Bazooka shelling; Villagers forced to sleep in underground shelters
5 Aug 1970	Four boys wounded by shellfire
16 Nov 1970	Plantation set on fire by shellfire

Lebanon will continue to honour its commitments and will serve in solving the Palestine problem
SAEB SALEM, LEBANESE PRIME MINISTER
8 JUNE 1973

Sea of Galilee

© Martin Gilbert

77

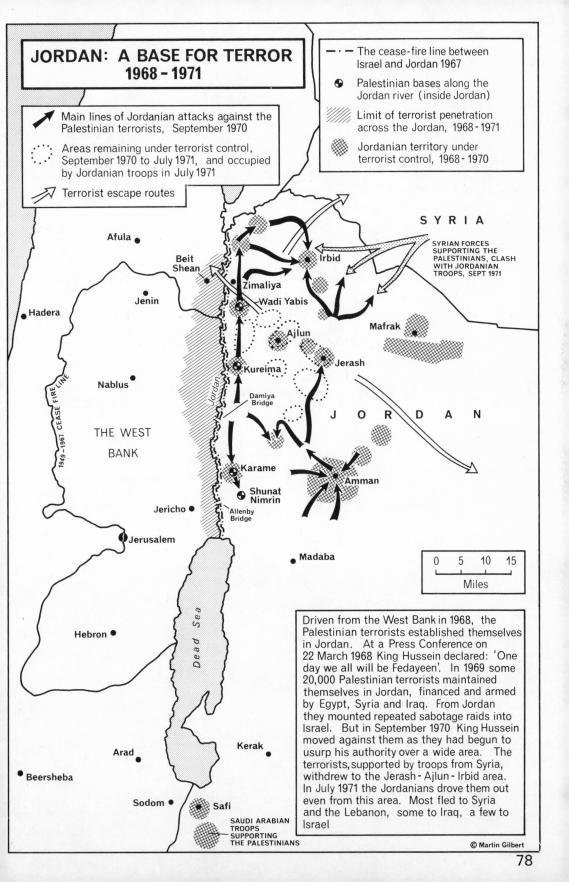

JORDAN: A BASE FOR TERROR
1968-1971

— · — The cease-fire line between Israel and Jordan 1967

⊕ Palestinian bases along the Jordan river (inside Jordan)

▨ Limit of terrorist penetration across the Jordan, 1968-1971

▨ Jordanian territory under terrorist control, 1968-1970

➤ Main lines of Jordanian attacks against the Palestinian terrorists, September 1970

⋰⋱ Areas remaining under terrorist control, September 1970 to July 1971, and occupied by Jordanian troops in July 1971

⇨ Terrorist escape routes

S Y R I A

SYRIAN FORCES SUPPORTING THE PALESTINIANS, CLASH WITH JORDANIAN TROOPS, SEPT 1971

Afula

Beit Shean

Jenin

Hadera

Zimaliya

Wadi Yabis

Irbid

Mafrak

Ajlun

Jerash

Nablus

Kureima

Damiya Bridge

J O R D A N

THE WEST BANK

1949-1967 CEASE FIRE LINE

Jordan

Karame

Shunat Nimrin

Allenby Bridge

Jericho

Jerusalem

Madaba

Hebron

Dead Sea

| 0 | 5 | 10 | 15 |

Miles

Driven from the West Bank in 1968, the Palestinian terrorists established themselves in Jordan. At a Press Conference on 22 March 1968 King Hussein declared: 'One day we all will be Fedayeen'. In 1969 some 20,000 Palestinian terrorists maintained themselves in Jordan, financed and armed by Egypt, Syria and Iraq. From Jordan they mounted repeated sabotage raids into Israel. But in September 1970 King Hussein moved against them as they had begun to usurp his authority over a wide area. The terrorists, supported by troops from Syria, withdrew to the Jerash - Ajlun - Irbid area. In July 1971 the Jordanians drove them out even from this area. Most fled to Syria and the Lebanon, some to Iraq, a few to Israel

Arad

Kerak

Beersheba

Sodom

Safi

SAUDI ARABIAN TROOPS SUPPORTING THE PALESTINIANS

© Martin Gilbert

THE WAR OF ATTRITION 1969-1970

During the war of attrition more than 200 Israeli soldiers were killed. The Egyptians did not issue casualty figures. As part of the cease-fire agreement, Egypt agreed not to place any missiles within a broad belt 20 miles west of the canal. But within two weeks of this agreement, she had built between 20 and 30 new sites, and moved up more than 500 missile war-heads

Damietta

Port Said

Kantara

Ismailia

BAR LEV LINE

Northern Sinai

Suez

Ras Sudr

Cairo

E G Y P T

Nile

Gulf of Suez

Southern Sinai

SAUDI ARABIA

Sharm el-Sheikh

Assiut

Hurghada

Red Sea

⊙ Principal Israeli fortifications of the 'Bar Lev' line under intense Egyptian bombardment, 1969-1970

▣ Principal military targets inside Egypt attacked by Israeli aircraft

⊕ Principal Israeli commando raids on Egyptian positions. Some of these raids were carried out by helicopter, some by sea

0   30
Miles

© Martin Gilbert

79

TERRORISM INSIDE ISRAEL: SOME EXAMPLES, 1969 – 1972

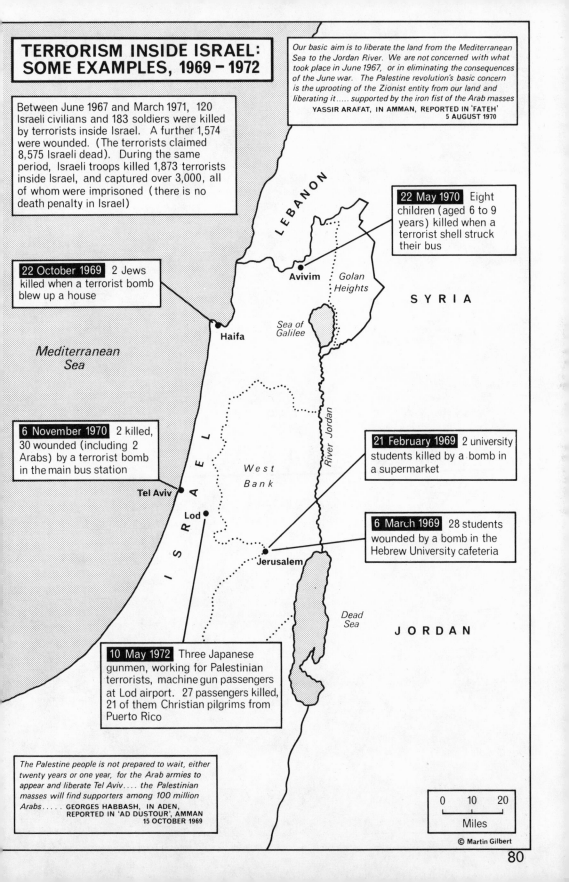

Our basic aim is to liberate the land from the Mediterranean Sea to the Jordan River. We are not concerned with what took place in June 1967, or in eliminating the consequences of the June war. The Palestine revolution's basic concern is the uprooting of the Zionist entity from our land and liberating it..... supported by the iron fist of the Arab masses

YASSIR ARAFAT, IN AMMAN, REPORTED IN 'FATEH'
5 AUGUST 1970

Between June 1967 and March 1971, 120 Israeli civilians and 183 soldiers were killed by terrorists inside Israel. A further 1,574 were wounded. (The terrorists claimed 8,575 Israeli dead). During the same period, Israeli troops killed 1,873 terrorists inside Israel, and captured over 3,000, all of whom were imprisoned (there is no death penalty in Israel)

22 May 1970 Eight children (aged 6 to 9 years) killed when a terrorist shell struck their bus

22 October 1969 2 Jews killed when a terrorist bomb blew up a house

LEBANON

Avivim

Golan Heights

S Y R I A

Sea of Galilee

Haifa

Mediterranean Sea

6 November 1970 2 killed, 30 wounded (including 2 Arabs) by a terrorist bomb in the main bus station

West Bank

River Jordan

21 February 1969 2 university students killed by a bomb in a supermarket

Tel Aviv

Lod

6 March 1969 28 students wounded by a bomb in the Hebrew University cafeteria

Jerusalem

Dead Sea

J O R D A N

10 May 1972 Three Japanese gunmen, working for Palestinian terrorists, machine gun passengers at Lod airport. 27 passengers killed, 21 of them Christian pilgrims from Puerto Rico

The Palestine people is not prepared to wait, either twenty years or one year, for the Arab armies to appear and liberate Tel Aviv.... the Palestinian masses will find supporters among 100 million Arabs..... **GEORGES HABBASH, IN ADEN, REPORTED IN 'AD DUSTOUR', AMMAN 15 OCTOBER 1969**

0   10   20

Miles

© Martin Gilbert

SOVIET TERRITORIAL ASPIRATIONS IN THE MIDDLE EAST, 1940

On 25 November 1940 the Soviet Government informed Nazi Germany that 'the centre' of what it described as Russia's 'territorial aspirations' was 'the area south of Baku and Batum in the general direction of the Persian Gulf'. Both the Germans and the Japanese accepted this definition of Soviet aims.

Territory included in a line drawn due south of Batum and Baku.

Territory included in a line drawn in the direction of the Persian Gulf.

Black Sea

Caspian Sea

Batum

Baku

THE SOVIET UNION

TURKEY

SYRIA

Mediterranean Sea

PALESTINE

Suez Canal

TRANSJORDAN

IRAQ

IRAN

EGYPT

Persian Gulf

Red Sea

SAUDI ARABIA

OMAN

SUDAN

YEMEN

ADEN PROTECTORATE

Arabian Sea

0   400
Miles

ADEN (British)
Bab-el-Mandeb Strait

SOCOTRA (British)

© Martin Gilbert

81

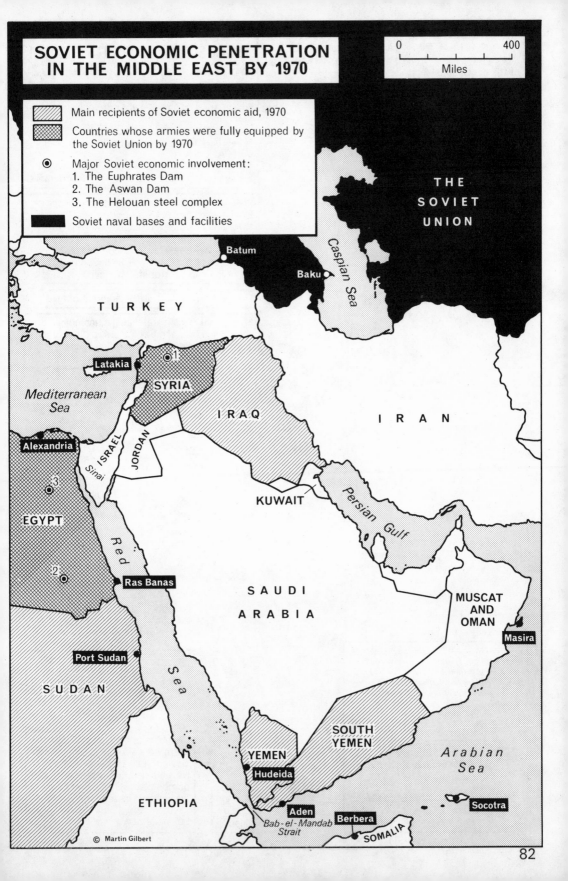

SOVIET ECONOMIC PENETRATION IN THE MIDDLE EAST BY 1970

0   400

Miles

Main recipients of Soviet economic aid, 1970

Countries whose armies were fully equipped by the Soviet Union by 1970

⊙   Major Soviet economic involvement:
1. The Euphrates Dam
2. The Aswan Dam
3. The Helouan steel complex

Soviet naval bases and facilities

THE SOVIET UNION

Batum

Baku

Caspian Sea

TURKEY

Latakia

⊙1

SYRIA

IRAQ

IRAN

Mediterranean Sea

Alexandria

ISRAEL

JORDAN

Sinai

KUWAIT

Persian Gulf

⊙3

EGYPT

Red Sea

⊙2

Ras Banas

SAUDI ARABIA

MUSCAT AND OMAN

Masira

Port Sudan

SUDAN

SOUTH YEMEN

Arabian Sea

YEMEN

Hudeida

Aden

Berbera

Socotra

ETHIOPIA

Bab - el - Mandab Strait

SOMALIA

© Martin Gilbert

82

PALESTINIAN TERRORISM BEYOND ISRAEL, 1969-1972

19 September 1972 The Agricultural Attaché of the Israeli Embassy killed by a letter bomb

6 February 1972 Dutch oil refineries sabotaged

8 February 1972 German aircraft engine plant sabotaged

16 February 1969 Crew member killed in attack on El Al plane
13 February 1970 47 passengers and crew of a Swissair plane killed by sabotage (17 were Israelis)

10 February 1970 An Israeli killed in an attack on El Al passengers in the airport
13 February 1970 Seven old Jews killed in an old peoples home
5 September 1972 Eleven Israeli athletes murdered at the Olympic Games. Two Germans and 5 terrorists also killed

5 August 1972 Italian oil refineries sabotaged

27 November 1969 Three Greeks, including a child, killed by a bomb at the El Al airlines office
26 December 1969 An Israeli killed in an attack on El Al passengers in the airport

London

Hamburg

Ravenstein

Zurich

Munich

Trieste

Mediterranean Sea

Athens

SYRIA
10,500

LEBANON
5,000

IRAQ
500

JORDAN
300

Cairo

ISRAEL

28 November 1971 Palestinian terrorists assassinate the Jordanian Prime Minister Wasfi Tal

LIBYA
2,000

EGYPT
2,300

Red Sea

We, the Syrians wish that the support of the resistance should not be in words but that it be practical and in deeds. The fidayun military activity springs from Syrian soil, and carries out successful operations with every assistance from Syria **ABD AL-HALIM KHADAM, SYRIAN FOREIGN MINISTER 23 SEPT 1971**

SUDAN

■ Approximate number of terrorists finding shelter in Arab countries, 1969-1972

◉ Terrorist activity outside Israel in which civilians (often non-Israelis) were murdered

As well as the specific terrorist acts shown here, there were a further nine successful hijackings between 1969 and 1972. As a result of the hijacking of a Lufthansa plane on 29 October 1972, the Arabs who had murdered members of the Israeli Olympic team were set free in Munich and flown to Libya. Between 1 and 11 November 1972 fourteen letter bombs were sent to Jewish addressees in London; one severely wounded a Jewish businessman

0   200
Miles

© Martin Gilbert

83

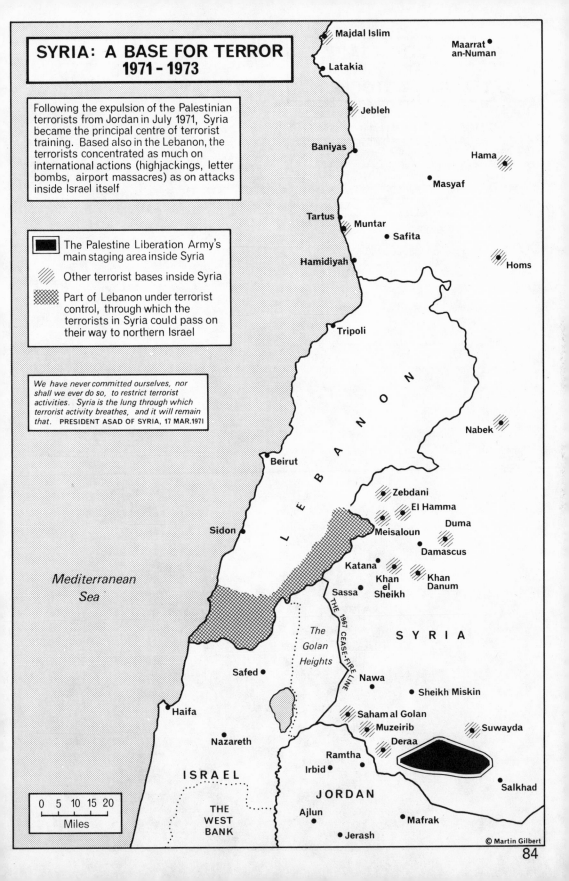

SYRIA: A BASE FOR TERROR
1971-1973

Following the expulsion of the Palestinian terrorists from Jordan in July 1971, Syria became the principal centre of terrorist training. Based also in the Lebanon, the terrorists concentrated as much on international actions (highjackings, letter bombs, airport massacres) as on attacks inside Israel itself

- The Palestine Liberation Army's main staging area inside Syria

- Other terrorist bases inside Syria

- Part of Lebanon under terrorist control, through which the terrorists in Syria could pass on their way to northern Israel

We have never committed ourselves, nor shall we ever do so, to restrict terrorist activities. Syria is the lung through which terrorist activity breathes, and it will remain that. **PRESIDENT ASAD OF SYRIA, 17 MAR.1971**

Majdal Islim

Maarrat an-Numan

Latakia

Jebleh

Baniyas

Hama

Masyaf

Tartus
Muntar
Safita

Homs

Hamidiyah

Tripoli

L E B A N O N

Nabek

Beirut

Zebdani

El Hamma

Duma

Meisaloun

Damascus

Sidon

Mediterranean Sea

Katana

Khan el Sheikh

Khan Danum

Sassa

S Y R I A

THE 1967 CEASE-FIRE LINE

The Golan Heights

Nawa

Sheikh Miskin

Safed

Saham al Golan

Muzeirib

Suwayda

Haifa

Deraa

Nazareth

Ramtha

Salkhad

Irbid

ISRAEL

JORDAN

Ajlun

Mafrak

THE WEST BANK

Jerash

0 5 10 15 20
Miles

© Martin Gilbert

84

ISRAELI RAIDS AGAINST TERRORIST BASES SEPTEMBER - OCTOBER 1972

0   10   20
Miles

On 5 September 1972 the Palestinian terror campaign reached a climax in the murder of eleven Israeli athletes at the Olympic village near Munich. In retaliation, Israeli forces struck at Palestinian bases in Syria and the Lebanon, attacking overland, by sea, and air

Israel 1949 to 1967

Administered by Israel, 1967 -

Palestinian terrorist bases attacked by Israeli forces in September 1972

Palestinian bases attacked in October 1972

Palestinian naval bases attacked during 1972

Latakia

Jebleh

Hama

Masyaf

Tartus
Muntar

Homs

Nahar el Bard

Tripoli

Mediterranean Sea

Beirut

L E B A N O N

Nabek

Zebdani

Ein Suhna   Ein Sahib

Rafid   Harna

Sidon

Dir el Ashayer   El   Duma
                       Hamma   Damascus

Nabatiya

Marjayoun   Hasbaya

Sarafand

Tulin   Bakifa

Juwaya
Tyre   El Khiam
Mahrune   Kabriha
Kafra   Majal Islam
Ras el Naba

Tibnin   Ainata   GOLAN
      Tiri   HEIGHTS   S Y R I A

Safed

Saham al Golan

Haifa   Suwayda

                                 Muzeirib
Nazareth

I S R A E L   Irbid   Deraa

                  J O R D A N

WEST
BANK   Ajlun

© Martin Gilbert

85

SOVIET ARMS SUPPLIES TO THE MIDDLE EAST
JANUARY 1970 – SEPTEMBER 1973

0   100   200
Miles

Countries receiving substantial arms supplies
from the Soviet Union, 1970-1973, and
attacking Israel on 6 October 1973

Country receiving arms from the Soviet
Union, and sending troops to the battlefield
against Israel during the October war

SOVIET   UNION

• Volgograd

Rostov

Nikolaeiev
Odessa   Kherson

Black Sea

Tiflis

Caspian Sea

Istanbul

Bosphorus

Dardanelles

Ankara

Trabzon

T U R K E Y

Izmir

Baku

Tabriz

• Teheran

CYPRUS

Aleppo

Latakia
Baniyas

SYRIA

Mosul

Baghdad

I R A Q

I R A N

Mediterranean
Sea

ARMS BY SEA

ARMS BY AIR

ARMS BY AIR

Port
Said

ISRAEL

JORDAN

Alexandria

Cairo

Suez

Sinai

E G Y P T

S A U D I
A R A B I A

Persian Gulf

Red
Sea

The total value of Soviet Arms Supplies to
Egypt and Syria between 1970 and 1973 was
estimated at £2000 million. This included
650 planes and 2500 tanks to Egypt, and
330 planes and 2000 tanks to Syria, all of
the most modern manufacture, and many
types not previously sent to Russia's
communist allies in eastern Europe. The
Soviet aid to Egypt and Syria included
hitherto highly secret anti-tank and anti-
aircraft missiles never before sent outside
the Soviet Union

© Martin Gilbert

86

THE BUILD UP TO WAR, 1972-1973

0 20 40 60
Miles

TURKEY

SYRIA

CYPRUS

Latakia

Baniyas

Tartus

10 August 1973 Israeli planes intercept a Libyan airliner en route to Iraq. Believing that the Palestinian terrorist leader George Habbash, is aboard, they force the plane to fly to Israel. Habbash was not on board and the intercepted plane was released after 2 hours, with no casualties

13 Sept 1973 In an air battle off the Syrian coast, one Israeli and at least eight Syrian planes shot down

In our coming battle, I will not be satisfied to liberate the land. Israel's arrogance and bluster, which has been going on for 23 years - all this must be terminated. As I have told them: I am ready to pay one million men as the price for this battle. But they too must be ready to pay a million men and more on their side
PRESIDENT SADAT AT THE MAY DAY RALLY IN ALEXANDRIA 1 MAY 1972

LEBANON

Beirut

Damascus

10 April 1973 Israeli commandos assassinate three Palestinian terrorist leaders

Haifa

5 October 1973 An Arab terrorist bomb kills an Israeli police officer

Tel Aviv
Lod

Amman

Jerusalem

Gaza

Port Said

Alexandria

Romani

El Arish

Negev

JORDAN

Ismailia

Bir Gafgafa

Cairo

I S R A E L

Suez

Uyun Musa

Eilat

Akaba

SAUDI ARABIA

E G Y P T

Sinai

Abu Rudeis

21 February 1973 Israeli planes force a Libyan civilian airliner to land in Sinai. It crash lands, killing 104 people, mostly Arabs. The Israelis had feared that the plane, flying over Israeli controlled territory, was on a terrorist sabotage mission to Tel Aviv (following several terrorist threats to bomb the city)

········ The 1949 cease-fire lines, Israel's borders 1949-1967

Sharm el-Sheikh

Red Sea

MILITARY BUDGETS	
EGYPT	$1,495 million (1971)
	$1,510 million (1972)
	$2,300 million (1973)
SYRIA	$ 176 million (1971)
	$ 206 million (1972)
	$ 400 million (1973)
ISRAEL	$1,295 million (1971)
	$1,285 million (1972)
	$1,444 million (1973)

© Martin Gilbert

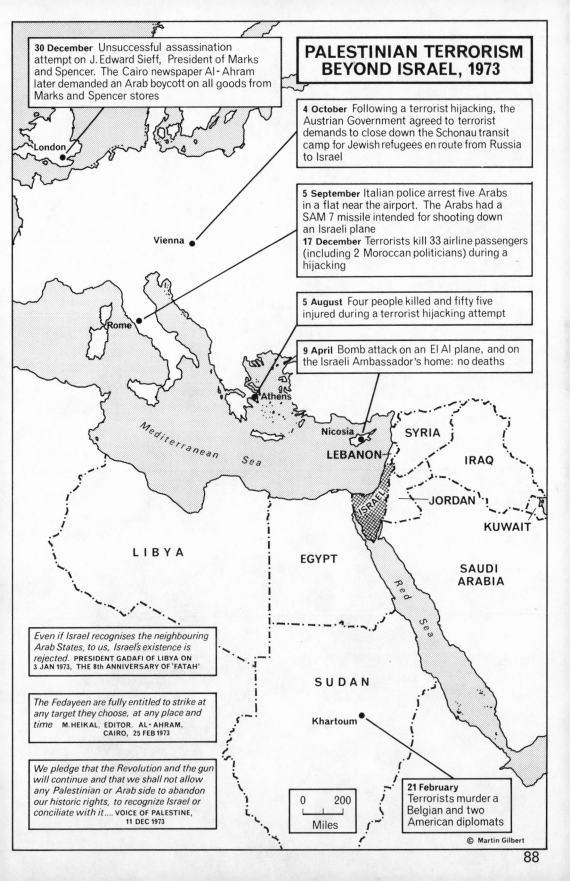

PALESTINIAN TERRORISM BEYOND ISRAEL, 1973

30 December Unsuccessful assassination attempt on J. Edward Sieff, President of Marks and Spencer. The Cairo newspaper Al-Ahram later demanded an Arab boycott on all goods from Marks and Spencer stores

4 October Following a terrorist hijacking, the Austrian Government agreed to terrorist demands to close down the Schonau transit camp for Jewish refugees en route from Russia to Israel

5 September Italian police arrest five Arabs in a flat near the airport. The Arabs had a SAM 7 missile intended for shooting down an Israeli plane
17 December Terrorists kill 33 airline passengers (including 2 Moroccan politicians) during a hijacking

5 August Four people killed and fifty five injured during a terrorist hijacking attempt

9 April Bomb attack on an El Al plane, and on the Israeli Ambassador's home: no deaths

London

Vienna

Rome

Athens

Nicosia

SYRIA

IRAQ

LEBANON

ISRAEL

JORDAN

KUWAIT

Mediterranean Sea

LIBYA

EGYPT

SAUDI ARABIA

Red Sea

SUDAN

Khartoum

Even if Israel recognises the neighbouring Arab States, to us, Israel's existence is rejected. **PRESIDENT GADAFI OF LIBYA ON 3 JAN 1973, THE 8th ANNIVERSARY OF 'FATAH'**

The Fedayeen are fully entitled to strike at any target they choose, at any place and time **M. HEIKAL, EDITOR, AL-AHRAM, CAIRO, 25 FEB 1973**

We pledge that the Revolution and the gun will continue and that we shall not allow any Palestinian or Arab side to abandon our historic rights, to recognize Israel or conciliate with it.... **VOICE OF PALESTINE, 11 DEC 1973**

21 February Terrorists murder a Belgian and two American diplomats

0   200
Miles

© Martin Gilbert

88

EUROPEAN DEPENDENCE ON ARAB OIL JANUARY – JUNE 1973

Sweden imported only 25% of its oil from Arab countries, as it relied principally on imports of refined oil from the Netherlands, as well as imports of oil from Iran, the Caribbean, Nigeria and the Soviet Union. The Belgian figure does not include refined oil imported from the Netherlands. The Netherlands figure covers only domestic consumption, and does not include oil re-exported to Sweden or Belgium.

■ European countries which imported over 50% of crude oil from the Arab world in the first six months of 1973 (with percentage shown in white).

Switzerland, not a major importer of crude oil, still depends heavily on the Middle East. The refined oil imported by Switzerland, coming from France, Italy and Holland, is mainly the product of Middle East crude. The same applies to imports of refined oil into Eire, Luxemburg, Norway and Greece.

0 100 200 300

Miles

NORWAY

SWEDEN

DENMARK

NETHERLANDS 68%

BELGIUM 69%

59%

WEST GERMANY 74%

SWITZ.

FRANCE 77%

GREAT BRITAIN 63%

EIRE

SPAIN 69%

ITALY 79%

North Sea

Adriatic Sea

Mediterranean Sea

GREECE

© Martin Gilbert

89

ARAB OIL PRESSURE SEPTEMBER – NOVEMBER 1973

Arab oil producing states reducing supplies. The figures show the daily production of barrels of oil (in millions of barrels) in September 1973, and the reduced figure for November 1973.

On 17 October 1973, eleven days after Egypt and Syria had attacked Israel, the Arab producing states agreed to cut supplies of oil to the oil importing states, hoping thereby to put political pressure on Israel.
On 4 November 1973 these same Arab states, with the exception of Iraq, agreed to a 25% cut in oil exports below the September level, in order to persuade the oil importers that Israel should be made to return to the 1967 cease fire lines

IRAQ
2 million
not reduced

KUWAIT
3·2 million
reduced to
2·2 million

SAUDI ARABIA
8·3 million
reduced to
6·2 million

DUBAI & OMAN
1 million
reduced to
0·8 million

ABU DHABI
1·4 million
reduced to
1·1 million

LIBYA
2·3 million
reduced to
1·7 million

QATAR
0·6 million
reduced to
0·45 million

ALGERIA
1 million
reduced to
0·8 million

NEUTRAL ZONE
0·6 million
reduced to
0·45 million

SYRIA
ISRAEL
EGYPT
OMAN
Dubai

Mediterranean Sea
Red Sea

Miles
0   250   500

© Martin Gilbert

90

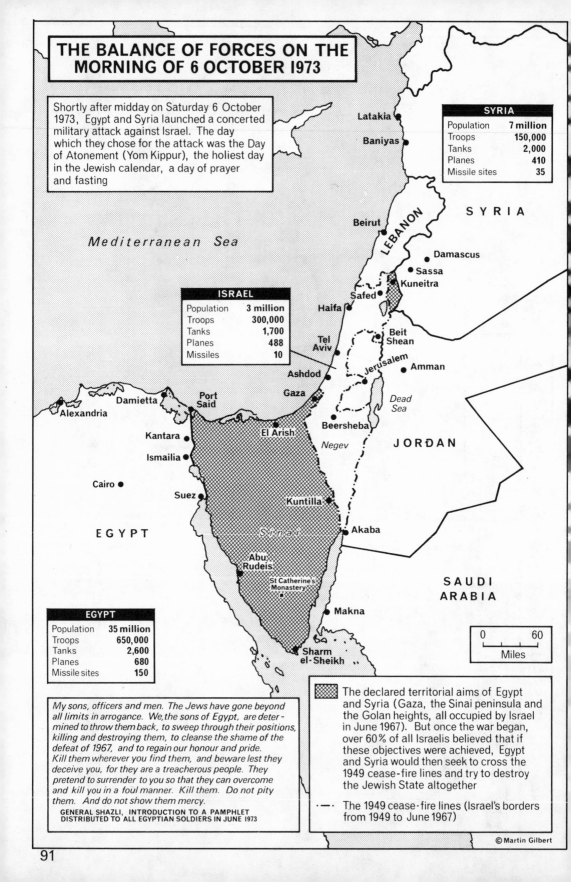

THE BALANCE OF FORCES ON THE MORNING OF 6 OCTOBER 1973

Shortly after midday on Saturday 6 October 1973, Egypt and Syria launched a concerted military attack against Israel. The day which they chose for the attack was the Day of Atonement (Yom Kippur), the holiest day in the Jewish calendar, a day of prayer and fasting

SYRIA	
Population	7 million
Troops	150,000
Tanks	2,000
Planes	410
Missile sites	35

ISRAEL	
Population	3 million
Troops	300,000
Tanks	1,700
Planes	488
Missiles	10

EGYPT	
Population	35 million
Troops	650,000
Tanks	2,600
Planes	680
Missile sites	150

Mediterranean Sea

Latakia
Baniyas
Beirut
LEBANON
SYRIA
Damascus
Sassa
Kuneitra
Safed
Haifa
Beit Shean
Tel Aviv
Jerusalem
Amman
Ashdod
Gaza
Dead Sea
Beersheba
JORDAN
Damietta
Port Said
Alexandria
Kantara
El Arish
Negev
Ismailia
Cairo
Suez
Kuntilla
Akaba
EGYPT
Sinai
Abu Rudeis
St Catherine's Monastery
SAUDI ARABIA
Makna
Sharm el-Sheikh

```
0        60
|___|___|
    Miles
```

My sons, officers and men. The Jews have gone beyond all limits in arrogance. We, the sons of Egypt, are deter-mined to throw them back, to sweep through their positions, killing and destroying them, to cleanse the shame of the defeat of 1967, and to regain our honour and pride. Kill them wherever you find them, and beware lest they deceive you, for they are a treacherous people. They pretend to surrender to you so that they can overcome and kill you in a foul manner. Kill them. Do not pity them. And do not show them mercy.

GENERAL SHAZLI, INTRODUCTION TO A PAMPHLET DISTRIBUTED TO ALL EGYPTIAN SOLDIERS IN JUNE 1973

The declared territorial aims of Egypt and Syria (Gaza, the Sinai peninsula and the Golan heights, all occupied by Israel in June 1967). But once the war began, over 60% of all Israelis believed that if these objectives were achieved, Egypt and Syria would then seek to cross the 1949 cease-fire lines and try to destroy the Jewish State altogether

-·-· The 1949 cease-fire lines (Israel's borders from 1949 to June 1967)

© Martin Gilbert

91

THE OCTOBER WAR, 6-24 OCTOBER 1973

0   60
Miles

Legend:

▬▬▬ The de-facto frontiers of Israel from 11 June 1967 to 6 October 1973

▲▲▲ Deepest penetration of Arab forces, 6-8 October

▨▨▨ Furthest limits of Israeli counter-attacks, 8-24 October

➤ Soviet arms supplies, 8-24 October

⇨ United States arms supplies, 12-24 October

⇦ Other Arab contributions of fighting troops and tanks

⊙ Syrian and Egyptian towns and ports bombed from the air or bombarded from the sea by Israeli forces

TURKEY

CYPRUS

SYRIA

Mint al Bayda
Latakia
Baniyas
Tartus
Homs

15,000 SYRIAN ARABS LEAVE AREA OF NEW ISRAELI OCCUPATION

LEBANON

Beirut

Damascus

230 TANKS AND CREWS FROM IRAQ

SOVIET MILITARY AID BY AIR & SEA; TOTAL VALUE 3,500 MILLION DOLLARS (TO EGYPT AND SYRIA)

SOVIET MILITARY AID

Jebel Baruch

A TOKEN FORCE OF MEN & VEHICLES FROM KUWAIT

UNITED STATES MILITARY AID BY AIR TOTAL VALUE 2,200 MILLION DOLLARS

Haifa

A TOKEN FORCE OF MEN & VEHICLES FROM SAUDI ARABIA

Lod

80 TANKS & CREWS FROM JORDAN

Ashdod

Amman

Gaza

Dead Sea

Damietta

Port Said

El Arish

Negev

JORDAN

Rosetta
Alexandria

Suez Canal

1,500 TROOPS FROM MOROCCO

Ismailia

ALGERIAN TROOPS STATIONED ON THE CANAL

Cairo

Sinai

Akaba

EGYPT

12-15 PLANES FROM IRAQ

Ras Zafarana

SAUDI ARABIA

Ras Gharib

When President Sadat said the other day that war must go on, and he is prepared to sacrifice a million men every year, one shudders not only at the thought of a million men giving away their lives, but that the head of a people can say it, that he can make this statement is something that makes one shudder. We don't want dead on our side, we have no joy in causing the death of others. But this people, small as it is, surrounded as it is by enemies, has decided to live. And if we have to pay the price for living, we have to pay it. **ISRAELI PREMIER GOLDA MEIR, 13 OCT**

Our forces will continue to pursue the enemy and strike at him.... until we restore our positions in our occupied land. After that, we shall continue until we liberate the whole land. **PRESIDENT ASSAD OF SYRIA 16 OCTOBER 1973**

The great historic fact is that they did have the opportunity to negotiate, they chose war. They could have talked. They decided to shoot. **ABBA EBAN ISRAELI FOREIGN MINISTER, 24 OCT**

© Martin Gilbert

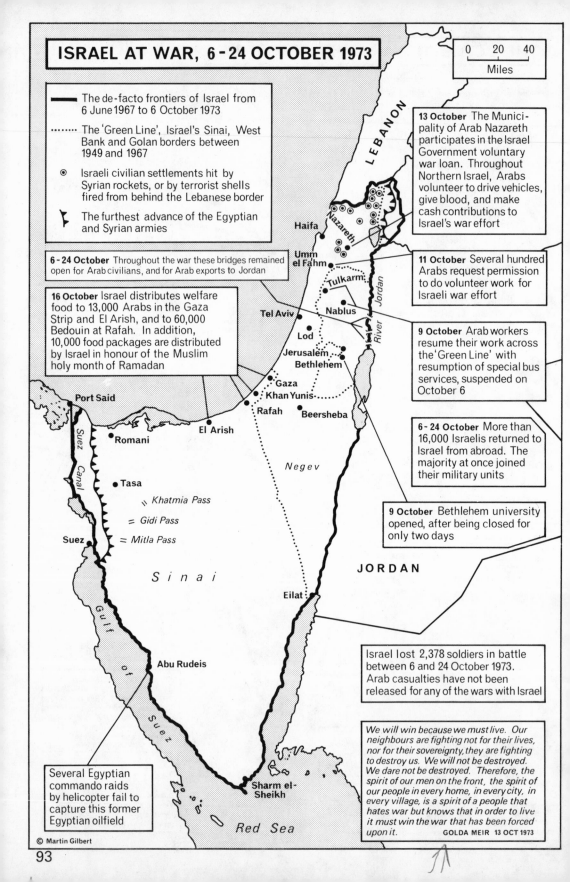

ISRAEL AT WAR, 6 - 24 OCTOBER 1973

Miles 0 20 40

— The de-facto frontiers of Israel from 6 June 1967 to 6 October 1973

······· The 'Green Line', Israel's Sinai, West Bank and Golan borders between 1949 and 1967

⊙ Israeli civilian settlements hit by Syrian rockets, or by terrorist shells fired from behind the Lebanese border

Ɣ The furthest advance of the Egyptian and Syrian armies

6 - 24 October Throughout the war these bridges remained open for Arab civilians, and for Arab exports to Jordan

16 October Israel distributes welfare food to 13,000 Arabs in the Gaza Strip and El Arish, and to 60,000 Bedouin at Rafah. In addition, 10,000 food packages are distributed by Israel in honour of the Muslim holy month of Ramadan

13 October The Municipality of Arab Nazareth participates in the Israel Government voluntary war loan. Throughout Northern Israel, Arabs volunteer to drive vehicles, give blood, and make cash contributions to Israel's war effort

11 October Several hundred Arabs request permission to do volunteer work for Israeli war effort

9 October Arab workers resume their work across the 'Green Line' with resumption of special bus services, suspended on October 6

6 - 24 October More than 16,000 Israelis returned to Israel from abroad. The majority at once joined their military units

9 October Bethlehem university opened, after being closed for only two days

LEBANON

Nazareth

Haifa

Umm el Fahm

Tulkarm

Nablus

Tel Aviv

Lod

Jerusalem

Bethlehem

Gaza

Khan Yunis

Rafah

Beersheba

River Jordan

JORDAN

Port Said

Suez Canal

El Arish

Romani

Tasa

Khatmia Pass

Gidi Pass

Mitla Pass

Suez

S i n a i

N e g e v

Eilat

Gulf of Suez

Abu Rudeis

Sharm el-Sheikh

Red Sea

Several Egyptian commando raids by helicopter fail to capture this former Egyptian oilfield

Israel lost 2,378 soldiers in battle between 6 and 24 October 1973. Arab casualties have not been released for any of the wars with Israel

We will win because we must live. Our neighbours are fighting not for their lives, nor for their sovereignty, they are fighting to destroy us. We will not be destroyed. We dare not be destroyed. Therefore, the spirit of our men on the front, the spirit of our people in every home, in every city, in every village, is a spirit of a people that hates war but knows that in order to live it must win the war that has been forced upon it.
GOLDA MEIR 13 OCT 1973

© Martin Gilbert

93

NORTHERN ISRAEL AND THE WAR, 6-24 OCTOBER 1973

Mount Hermon

Metulla
Misgav Am
Kfar Giladi
Margaliyot
Manara
Kfar Yuval
Kiryat Shmona
Beit Hillel

Majdal Shams
Dan
Hagoshrim
Maasada
Bukata
Kfar Szold
Shamir

El Rom

Merom Golan
Kuneitra

Ein Zivan

SYRIA

Yiftah

LEBANON

Avivim
Yiron
Sde Eliezer
Ayelet Hashahar
Mahanayim

Gadot

Kafar Naffakh

Khushniye

Tel Faris

0 1 2 3 4
Miles

Rosh Pina

Golan Heights

Jordan

ISRAEL

Ramot

Ramat Magshimim

Legend

— · — The frontiers of Israel on 6 October 1973

·········· The cease-fire line between Israel and Syria, 1949-1967

⬐ The general direction of the Syrian advance, 6-8 October

⊙ Israeli settlements on the Golan Heights, overrun by Syrian tanks, 6-8 October

■ Israeli towns and settlements hit by shells and rockets from Syria and the Lebanon, 6-24 Oct.

☐ Druze villages bombed and shelled by Syrians 6-24 October

☀ Places where Syrian troops murdered Israeli soldiers after they had been captured

Ginossar
Sea of Galilee
Tiberias
Ein Gev
Afik
Degania

JORDAN

One Israeli was killed and 16 wounded as a result of shelling from Syria and rocket attacks from the Lebanon, 6-24 October. Twelve Druze were killed by Syrian shelling and bombing in the same period and 250 Druze houses damaged. Both Israeli and Druze settlements lost substantial wooded and orchard areas as a result of fires started during these attacks

The Syrians captured 119 Israeli soldiers between 6 and 8 October 1973. Of these, 42 were subsequently found dead, having been killed after they had been taken prisoner. The Syrians refused to give the Red Cross the names of the Israeli prisoners in their hands, or to allow the Red Cross to visit them, until 28 February 1974, when they announced that they held 62 prisoners, and that 15 more had died while in Syrian hands

© Martin Gilbert

THE RED SEA BLOCKADE OCTOBER-DECEMBER 1973

ΛΛΛ The Egyptian naval blockade
October - December 1973

Israeli shipping routes cut by the Egyptian blockade

At the outset of the October War, Egyptian naval forces blockaded the Red Sea, thus halting all Israeli sea borne trade with Iran, India, Australasia and the Far East. The blockade was kept in force for almost two months after the cease fire of 24 October. By 12 November nine merchant ships and three oil tankers were stranded in Eilat and eleven ships en route to Eilat were forced to turn back. The alternate route was via the Cape of Good Hope, a journey of over 12,000 miles from Socotra to Ashdod. The Red Sea blockade was finally lifted by 13 December

Black Sea

Caspian Sea

SOVIET UNION

TURKEY

Mus

Malatya

Lake Van

Tabriz

Iskenderun

Aleppo

Mosul

SYRIA

IRAQ

Teheran

IRAN

CYPRUS

Mediterranean Sea

Baghdad

Ashdod

ISRAEL

JORDAN

Bandar Shahpur

Cairo

Eilat

Persian Gulf

Sharja

SAUDI

Abu Dhabi

EGYPT

Medina

Yenbo

Ras Banas

ARABIA

MUSCAT AND OMAN

Mecca

Jidda

Red Sea

Port Sudan

SOUTH YEMEN

FROM IRAN

SUDAN

Massawa

YEMEN

FROM INDIA, AUSTRALASIA AND THE FAR EAST

Socotra

Aden

Indian Ocean

ETHIOPIA

Bab-el-Mandeb Strait

FROM EAST AFRICA

0 100 200
Miles

© Martin Gilbert

95

MIDDLE EAST ARMS SUPPLIES: SCUD

'Scud' range if fired from Ismailia

'Scud' range if fired from a line 50 miles east of the Suez Canal

'Scud' range if fired from the pre-1967 cease-fire line (Israel's borders from 1949 to 1967)

········ Israel's Sinai border, 1949-1967

On 2 November 1973 it was announced in Washington that Egypt had received Soviet surface-to-surface missiles with a range of 160 miles. These 'Scud' missiles can be armed with either high explosive warheads, or nuclear warheads. Washington later confirmed that Syria had also been sent 'Scud' missiles from the Soviet Union. These, if fired from Sassa, could hit Beersheba

Mediterranean Sea

Beirut

LEBANON

SYRIA

Damascus

Sassa

Safed

Haifa

Afula

Irbid

Tel Aviv

Jerusalem

Amman

Ashdod

Gaza

Arad

Beersheba

JORDAN

El Arish

Negev

Suez Canal

50 miles

Ismailia

Cairo

Suez

Mitla Pass

Sinai

Maan

EGYPT

Eilat

SAUDI ARABIA

0 10 20 30 40 50

Miles

© Martin Gilbert

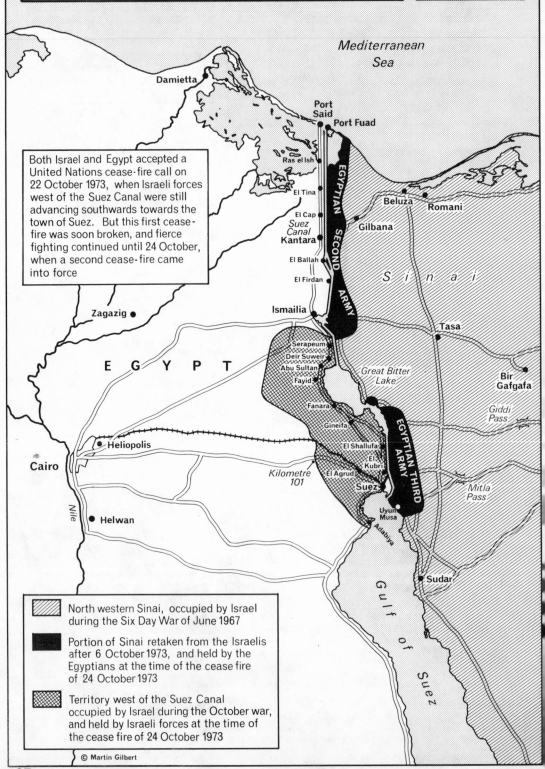

THE EGYPTIAN FRONT AT THE CEASE FIRE OF 24 OCTOBER 1973

0 5 10 15 20
Miles

Mediterranean Sea

Damietta

Port Said
Port Fuad

Ras el Ish

Both Israel and Egypt accepted a United Nations cease-fire call on 22 October 1973, when Israeli forces west of the Suez Canal were still advancing southwards towards the town of Suez. But this first cease-fire was soon broken, and fierce fighting continued until 24 October, when a second cease-fire came into force

El Tina

El Cap
Suez Canal
Kantara

Beluza
Romani

Gilbana

El Ballah

El Firdan

S i n a i

Zagazig

Ismailia

Tasa

E G Y P T

Serapeum
Deir Suweir
Abu Sultan
Fayid

Great Bitter Lake

Bir Gafgafa

Giddi Pass

Fanara

Gineifa

Heliopolis

El Shallufa

EGYPTIAN THIRD ARMY

Cairo

Kilometre 101

El Agrud

El Kubri

Suez

Mitla Pass

Nile

Helwan

Uyun Musa

Adabiya

Sudar

Gulf of Suez

North western Sinai, occupied by Israel during the Six Day War of June 1967

Portion of Sinai retaken from the Israelis after 6 October 1973, and held by the Egyptians at the time of the cease fire of 24 October 1973

Territory west of the Suez Canal occupied by Israel during the October war, and held by Israeli forces at the time of the cease fire of 24 October 1973

© Martin Gilbert

THE SYRIAN FRONT AT THE CEASE FIRE
OF 24 OCTOBER 1973

0   5   10
Miles

– – – Border between Israel and Syria, 1949-1967

Territory of the State of Israel from the cease fire after the Six-Day War of June 1967, until the Syrian attack on 6 October 1973

Syrian territory held by Israel at the cease fire of 24 October 1973

Mediterranean Sea

Beirut

Barr Elias

L E B A N O N

Damascus

Sidon

Katana

Rasheiya

Mount Hermon

Hasbaya

Marjayoun

Kiswe

Mazraat Beit Jann

Sassa

Tyre

Jubbata

Kanakir

Kiryat Shmona

Khan Erenbe

S Y R I A

Bint Jubail

Kuneitra

Jeba

Golan

Kafr Shams

Es Sanamein

Heights

El Harra

Rosh Pina

Khushniye

Jasim

Safed

Rafid

Butmiye

Sea of Galilee

Ramat Magshimim

Sheikh Miskin

Tiberias

Saham al Golan

ISRAEL

Yarmuk

Nazareth

During the fighting 15,000 Syrian civilians fled from the area shown in black

Deraa

Afula

Irbid

Jordan

Beit Shean

J O R D A N

© Martin Gilbert

ISRAELI AND EGYPTIAN DISENGAGEMENT PROPOSALS NOVEMBER 1973

0 10 20 30 40 50
Miles

ISRAELI PROPOSAL

1. Israeli forces to withdraw altogether from the west bank of the Suez Canal

2. The Egyptian second army to remain on the east bank of the canal

3. The Egyptian third army to withdraw to the west bank of the canal, but to be replaced by a small Egyptian police force, larger than a token force

4. All Israeli troops to withdraw to a line some ten kilometres west of the 1967-1973 cease-fire line along the canal, keeping the passes under Israeli control

EGYPTIAN PROPOSAL

1. All Israeli forces to be withdrawn east of a line from El Arish to Sharm el-Sheikh, with further withdrawals to be a matter for the Peace Conference

— · — The 1949 cease-fire line, Israel's de-facto border, 1949-1967

⊙ Israeli settlements in Sinai, established between 1967 and 1973

Mediterranean Sea

THE WEST BANK

R. Jordan

Tel Aviv

Amman

Port Said

Jerusalem

Gaza
Dikla

Dead Sea

El Arish

Rafiah

Sadot

JORDAN

Nahal Yam

Nahal Sinai

Nizana

Bir Gafgafa

Kusseima

Giddi Pass

Cairo

Kilometre 101

Mitla Pass

Sinai

Kuntilla

EGYPT

Nile

OIL FIELDS

Eilat
Taba

Akaba

OIL FIELDS

Neviot

SAUDI ARABIA

Gulf of Suez

Shalhevet

St.Catherine's Monastery

Di-Zahav

Tor

Makna

Negotiations for the disengagement of forces began at Kilometre 101 on 11 November 1973. At first the Israeli plan seemed to be acceptable to the Egyptians as a basis for limited mutual withdrawals. On 28 November, however, after the Arab summit conference at Algiers, the Egyptians produced a wide-ranging plan for a major Israeli evacuation of Sinai. This, the Israelis claimed, could only be decided at the peace conference planned to open at Geneva on 18 December. The negotiations thereupon broke down

Ophir
Ras Mohammed

Red Sea

© Martin Gilbert

THE DISENGAGEMENT OF FORCES ON THE SUEZ FRONT, JANUARY – MARCH 1974

0 5 10 15
Miles

Mediterranean Sea

Port Said
Port Fuad

Romani

SUEZ CANAL

Kantara West

ZONE B

ZONE C

E G Y P T

ZONE A

Ismailia
Lake Timsah

Great Bitter Lake

Fayid

Little Bitter Lake

SUEZ CANAL

On 18 January 1974 Egypt and Israel signed an agreement on the Disengagement of Forces, the disengagement to be completed 'not later than 40 days' after it began. The last Israeli forces left the western side of the Suez Canal on 21 Feb. The disengagement was finally completed on 5 March. Within three weeks there was a major breach of the agreement by Egypt, which moved artillery pieces in excess of the agreement to the east of the Suez Canal. After Israeli protest the extra artillery was withdrawn (4 April)

Perhaps I am mistaken, but in my estimation their faces are truly turned towards peace.
M. DAYAN, ISRAELI DEFENCE MINISTER 19 JAN 1974

Suez

Port Tewfik
Uyun Musa

Mitla Pass

Adabiya

S i n a i

—— 'A' Line
—·—·— 'B' Line
– – – 'C' Line
▨ United Nations Emergency Force

Gulf of Suez

Ras Sudar

Under this Agreement, Egypt and Israel agreed to 'scrupulously observe the cease fire on land, sea and air', and to refrain 'from all military or para-military actions against each other'. All Egyptian forces in Sinai had to be deployed west of Line 'A'. All Israeli forces had to withdraw east of Line 'C'. A United Nations force had then to move into the zone between Lines 'A' and 'B'. Egypt agreed to limit the size of its forces to 7,000 men, 30 tanks and 36 heavy artillery pieces between Line 'A' and the Suez Canal. Israel agreed to a similar limitation between Lines 'B' and 'C'. Egypt also agreed to place its missile sites in such a way as to give only defensive cover to her own forces

© Martin Gilbert

100

THE ARAB-ISRAELI CONFLICT: AIMS AND OPINIONS NOVEMBER 1973 - MARCH 1974

The war is not over yet. We must admit that our territory has not yet been liberated and we have another fight before us for which we must prepare. **GENERAL GAMASSY, EGYPTIAN CHIEF OF STAFF, 4 MARCH 1974**

On 2 February 1974 the Egyptians announced that they had begun work to open the Suez Canal. But simultaneously with the disengagement of the Egyptian and Israeli forces in Sinai, the Syrians began to bombard Israeli military positions and civilian settlements on the Golan heights. On 3 February 1974 the Syrian Foreign Minister, A.H. Khaddam, announced that Syria was carrying out 'continued and real war of attrition... keeping Israel's reserves on active duty and paralysing its economy'. Throughout March 1974 the Syrians insisted that there could be no negotiations with Israel until Israel withdrew completely from the Golan Heights. On 31 March it was stated in Washington that a 'foreign legion' serving inside Syria included units from Kuwait, Morocco and Saudi Arabia, as well as North Korean pilots and a Cuban armoured brigade with over 100 tanks

The Soviet Union and Syria re-affirm that the establishment of a durable and just peace cannot be achieved in the Middle East unless Israel withdraws from all occupied territories, and the legitimate rights of the Palestinians are restored. **SOVIET FOREIGN MINISTER GROMYKO AND SYRIAN PRESIDENT ASSAD, JOINT STATEMENT 7 MARCH 1974**

LEBANON

Beirut

Damascus

Kuneitra

SYRIA

The Golan Heights

Netanya

Tel Aviv

R. Jordan

ISRAEL

Mediterranean Sea

JORDAN

Amman

Jerusalem

Gaza

Dead Sea

SAUDI ARABIA

Port Said

Beersheba

El Arish

Negev

Suez Canal

Bir Gafgafa

Sinai

Cairo

Suez

Eilat

Akaba

E G Y P T

Gulf of Suez

Gulf of Eilat

Abu Rudeis

--·- The 1949 cease-fire lines (Israel's borders 1949 - 1967)

Occupied by Israeli forces in June 1967

The front lines at the ceasefire of October 1973

The zone of disengagement in Sinai, March 1974

Sharm el-Sheikh

Palestine is not only part of the Arab homeland but also a basic part of South Syria. We consider it our right and duty to insist that Palestine should remain a free part of our Arab homeland and of our Arab Syrian country. **PRESIDENT ASSAD OF SYRIA, 8 MARCH 1974**

I am not for staying 20 kilometres from the Canal. I do not see in Abu Rudeis, and in oil, the final security line for Israel - although there is oil there - because it means also control of the Suez Canal. I can see all the reasons for wanting control on the Gulf of Eilat, but I cannot think we will have peace with Egypt while we control not only the entrance to Eilat but also the entrance to Suez. **M.DAYAN, ISRAELI DEFENCE MINISTER, 10 MARCH 1974**

We stick to our stand that Israel should withdraw from all Arab territories she occupied since June 1967, and say that there can be no peace in this area without complete withdrawal. We also need not say that Arab Jerusalem, that precious jewel on the forehead of this homeland, will never and under no circumstances come under any sovereignty other than absolute Arab sovereignty. **KING HUSSEIN OF JORDAN, 2 DEC 1973**

For the Syrians, the occupied territories means not only the Golan Heights, but Jerusalem, and even Tel Aviv. **U.S. SECRETARY OF STATE, HENRY KISSINGER, 11 MARCH 1974**

....we will not descend from the Golan, we will not partition Jerusalem, we will not return Sharm el-Sheikh, and we will not agree that the distance between Netanya and the border shall be 18 kilometres.... But if we want a Jewish State we have to be prepared to compromise on territory. **GOLDA MEIR, ISRAELI PRIME MINISTER, 29 DEC 1973**

.... the talk in Israel about a demilitarized Sinai should stop. If they want a demilitarized Sinai, I shall be asking for a demilitarized Israel. **PRESIDENT SADAT OF EGYPT, 'TIME' MAGAZINE, 25 MARCH 1974**

© Martin Gilbert